Leadership Journey of a Project Manager

9 STORIES, 9 TOOLS, 1 VISION

JOHN ROBERT

"*When you are inspired by some great purpose, some extraordinary project, all your thoughts break their bounds. Your mind transcends limitations, your consciousness expands in every direction, and you find yourself in a new, great and wonderful world. Dormant forces, faculties, and talents come alive, and you discover yourself to be a greater person by far than you ever dreamt yourself to be.*"

Patañjali - the compiler of the Yoga Sutra, (2nd c. BCE)

My tribute to A. P. J. Abdul Kalam

Table of contents

Preface

"The journey of a thousand miles begins with one step," according to Lao Tzu; here there are nine steps we could take in the journey of leadership. I am thrilled, not only for that you have chosen to read the book but for traveling along with you on this transformation journey. The project community has gone for a long haul in the management track and indeed produced the most needed efficiency and results in the industrial era. Now in the information era, it is time for us to switch on to the leadership paradigm to create not only efficient but excellent results.

Storytelling is the most powerful way to put ideas into the world today, according to Robert McAfee Brown. I too have used several stories in the book to illustrate case studies in projects. *All characters and events depicted in this book are entirely fictitious. Any similarity to actual events or persons, living or dead, is not only purely coincidental but is a fact of real-life experience in projects, it means that many organizations are suffering from these common syndromes.* No animals were harmed during the making of these stories, but there is indeed leadership suffering. The focus here is on becoming a cure for this. I am sure this book will be a part of the solution and not part of the problem. This book is meant to be dynamic, hence please share your success stories, that can get as a part of the learning curve of fellow leaders.

I had the opportunity to be a part of multiple projects for the last two decades, both massive construction projects as well as the research and development projects, in a weak matrix as well as projectized organizations. While it remains a continuous learning endeavor, what I have figured out is that some simple tools help to create tremendous visibility, hands-on problem-solving, and to create the change which every project manager is looking forward to. Among those, I was thinking of choosing the best, to give that as a package for every project manager to use to create far superior results in their projects. This is my humble effort to compile these simple yet essential tools and bundle them as a toolkit. There is something more to it. This becomes unforgettable as all these tools are connected with numbers. While it is simple, it is also easy for one to remember, hence practicing in a real-world scenario seldom becomes difficult. One can instantaneously upgrade their skills as a project leader 2.0 like counting one, two, and three, just like that!

Former President of India, APJ Abdul Kalam, is an excellent example of the height which can be attained by a project manager. He was well-regarded as a scientist and teacher. However, a more in-depth look into his career reveals that indeed he was a project manager as well for most of his career. Not merely a target-oriented project manager, but also a leader who could connect to the people and inspire them to act. There are several examples in his life in which he was able to communicate the vision undoubtedly, bring people together to work towards an objective. He was also able to connect to the people at their intimate level and established rapport. He was a great example and an inspiration for me and this book. He was the one who looked at the results but also on the causes, which can break boundaries, and take the project leadership to the next level. He went on to become the president of the world's largest democracy. What a journey for a project manager with a humble beginning!

• Project management is essential for project success
• Project leadership is essential for the sustained success of projects

While these tools apply to every project manager, these are also applicable to our life project. Through this journey, I aimed to create influential project leaders, empowered teams, and excellence in results in today's information era. That is my intention in this book. May the power be with you.

John Robert

Jan 2019

Introduction

In one sense, 'everyone is a project manager' in an organization. The one who has planned for a vacation has already been in the role of a project manager. When you are planning a vacation, what do we start with? We begin with the destination. Beginning with the end in mind is the first step in vacation planning. For a project, the scope document indicates the product or services that need to be created at the end. Once the destination is fixed, then we start planning and booking resorts and hotels. Then planning out our journey from a point to another point. All these intermediate points in projects are milestones. All the reservation which is happening is planning. We enjoy the vacation with the process of planning, organizing, execution, control, and closeout. So, everyone is a project manager and a project manager becomes a better manager by using a set of appropriate tools.

In reality, sometimes we feel that there is a need for superpowers to project managers to manage the complex situations of the projects. This might include conditions like

•   Holding a crystal ball to look at the future and precisely estimate the completion time of the project
•   A stroke of a magic wand to bring together the teams with their own priorities and make the project a single common priority
•   Turn around a failing project overnight
•   Lead the people who are not directly reporting
•   Champion the systems in a chaotic unsystematic ecosystem

1

- Be a change catalyst in change-averse conditions
- Doing more with Less
- Complete a project with less cost and deliver far superior quality "simultaneously."

We are witnessing that, ironically, some of these expectations coming up from the organization with lower project management maturity. The weak matrix organizations where the project managers are disempowered and at the same time expected to do miracles. We recognize that the project management 'breed' is something which is about driving something which is dealing with unknown aspects that are vulnerable and consistently changing. The need is to inculcate power to handle the vulnerabilities of a project, something like a superpower.

When it comes to Superpowers, we tend to associate that with either God or Superheroes immediately. Who are superheroes? They are ordinary people who can do extraordinary things with their specialized tools and skills. Spider-Man's Web-Shooters, Batman's Batarangs, Captain America's Shield, Ghost Rider's Hellfire Enchanted Chain, Green Arrow's Bow & Arrows, Green Lantern's Power Ring, Iron Man's Suit, and Thor's "Mjolnir" Hammer - all of them are inseparable tools of them and without which the superhero often is powerless.

Whether it is a weak matrix or a balanced matrix or a strong matrix, a project leader with a set of tools can become a superhero in her own sense in his own ecosystem. This is an effort to upgrade the project leader by providing appropriate toolsets. These are nine simple tools that have been included here, will make a project leader create extraordinary results in project environments. These tools are selected based on the challenges of today's project environment. The tools that matter makes the project leader exceed the performance of an average project manager.

When David faced Goliad, he had a simple tool only, yet very appropriate to the need of the hour, which he used to conquer the situation. In the game of success vs. failure, many times having the right tools helps a lot. Project managers as well, like a small boy who was chosen from the Israelites. Project managers are the chosen ones to handle Goliath kind of significant problems and lead the team. Having the right set of the toolkit is the one that prepares them to handle such a situation.

The military vocabulary VUCA is a commonly used acronym in the business world. Volatility, Uncertainty, Complexity, and Ambiguity are the inherent DNA of any project. Handling such complexity calls for extreme agility and leadership skills. Particularly in the knowledge era, where there is the lion's share of cognitive projects compared to the brick and mortar projects.

Project management is the application of best practices in initiating, planning, executing, controlling, and closing out of the projects to producing specific products or services. Yet in the real world, just planning and organizing may not be adequate for one to thrive in a complex situation. In today's context, a project manager is almost like a miniature CEO of her project and is being responsible for all the good, ugly, and unfortunate that happened to the project. The contribution of a project manager in today's business is more than mere planning and organizing. Project

Management has become an art of influencing and converging diverse groups towards a common objective. It is more to do with anticipating issues that shape conditions, working on various alternatives and opportunities, and controlling chaos in the system. It is about managing variables in the undercurrent of change and restructures. This calls for a lot of skills and tools needed to not only survive but to thrive in complex projects.

Part I:

Project Leadership

A New Breed of Leadership

The project ecosystem itself has undergone a sea of change. Most of the changes are because of the shift from the industrial age to the knowledge era. Two decades ago, the situation was a bit different, most of the projects are of industrial nature, and the predominant skills requirement is the power of machines and the exertion of muscles with the machine. Today in the information era, projects are having more share of cognitive work and technology. Some of the popular examples are nanotechnology, biotechnology, quantum mechanics, and the ever-growing information technology-related projects. These are the only tip of the iceberg, yet many start-ups, innovation programs targeting at solving the unresolved problem finding the solution for unmet needs. Most of the projects are around finding an answer to the quest the human race had for a long time. These projects are from an unchartered tertiary and the issues which are being dealt with today are that we do not have precedence or a prototype to quickly fix them. That doesn't mean that the industrial age projects are behind us, we continue to create megastructures, build infrastructure, create extensive powerhouses for the businesses to operate efficiently. However, even in these projects, human intelligence is more valuable than that of manpower or machine power. Hence in today's project scenario, project leadership is more about managing the intellectual capacity of people, and soft skills are a vital part of doing that.

Hence there is a need for an altogether new skillset, toolset, and mindset to lead a project in the right direction. Initially, the project managers played the role of coordinators, now

7

need to drive the projects from the front. Project managers become frontrunners and owners of the project, they take vital decisions, solve problems, and create winning teams and foster an enabling culture in managing value from today's business ecosystem. There is a significant contribution of a project manager eminent to a greater extent in today's project. The success or failure today depends on not only the technical skills it also equally depends on the leadership skills which every project manager or project leader should possess.

We can also look at getting things done in brick and mortar projects and cognitive-complex knowledge projects having a different mode of operation. Getting things done in a brick and mortar project is maximizing the efficiency of the equipment that was used to create the scope of the project. In the knowledge of this project, it is more to do with how to get the maximum from the human potential. While the former is about maintaining the machines and keeping them in excellent condition, the latter is about keeping the intellectual workforce motivated to deliver the maximum potential.

There is a paradigm shift in the mindset of the people who are engaged in projects. The knowledge workforce has a passion for doing things and achieving results. This, of course, includes the project managers themselves. Project teams are scattered around the world. There is so much interdependency between the units which are operating from every corner of the globe. There are subject matter experts; there are offshoring to the external partners, and indeed, there are competitors. Hence the bandwidth in which a project manager needs to operate has widened a lot comparing to what used to be a while ago. Each part of the world has its own culture to deal with, so the project manager to influence entire stakeholders and then bring everybody together to align to attain the objective of the project is a vital factor for the success of projects today.

First of all, let us see why a shift is needed in the way the projects are governed. There are three factors which we might consider, as a sign of the necessity for us to move more towards a new way of working.

Temporary Endeavor

A project is considered a temporary endeavor that is having a definite start and a definite end. Project teams were also treated as temporary teams, which come together for a specific project and then disseminate after completion of the project. This, however, can be linked to the genesis of managing projects, from the beginning of the discipline, the Apollo moon mission as well as various military operations. Yet, is the temporary endeavor still a valid 'tag' of projects?

Maybe, maybe not

Today projects and the portfolio has become the cornerstone of every industry. Projects are needed in order to create new facilities, build capabilities, development, and launch new products. In one sense project teams are permanent and are continuously engaged in project activities. I have been in the industry for the past two decades, creating capacity and innovating new products. There has been and never a dull moment in my career. Today project teams become an indispensable part of the industry, and they have projects one after another to achieve the strategic intent of the business. While an individual project is temporary, the teams that execute that are being engaged in a continuum. There is a need for us to move more towards leadership, which is necessary for us to sustain the momentum between project to project with the interest of the team which is engaged in such endeavors.

Machine Dependence of The Project

Conventionally, the project depends more on earthmovers and heavy machinery, to create the infrastructure. While handling the machines is a vital skill, then the focus is on maximizing the efficiency of those to get the best out of them. Is this efficiency orientation, which is meant for machines are still valid in today's projects?

Maybe, maybe not

The machines need to be operating continuously without interruption to keep them running at their best productivity. When it comes to human resources is not the efficiency but the effectiveness which makes a difference. A passionate individual is much more productive than an average employee. The teams which have absolute clarity on the purpose of the project aligned with the vision make the job faster than the other. Hence the voluntary engagement of the people makes a significant difference in a project, applying all that meant for machines-driven projects may not be the best way of managing the teams going forward. Machines don't need to be motivated, but to be maintained well to work efficiently. People require no maintenance, but latitude to unleash the full potential of them. The use of inspiration for machines and maintenance for people is a no-brainer.

Cause and Effect

Today projects more relying on the cognitive capacity of the people. There is no clear correlation between the effort and result, in other words, cause and effect. For instance, while doing research and development, a product might get clinched in the first iteration or would take multiple iterations for a scientist to get to that point. Innovation requires various hypotheses to be proved or disproved to come up with the concept that yields a new product. In the past, when projects are done through machines, the cause and effect had a linear relationship, one can accurately estimate how much dirt can be moved, for example, by an earthmover per hour. Hence the efficiency of that equipment determined the project progress predominantly. Nowadays, project managers were not able to ascertain how many iterations it will take to conclude a concept. Does the measurement of effort be an accurate reflection of the progress of the project anymore?

Maybe, maybe not

More and more projects become iterative. While machines are still used in projects, they only augment the intellectual capability of the people who are involved in the project. The company which innovates faster and adapts to the rapid technology obsolescence thrives in the fiercely competitive market space. These innovations or technology adaptations cannot be made by machines, and fundamentally are driven by the cognitive workforce. While to a certain extent efficiency orientation can be applied for people, the real success comes from keeping them motivated and making them share the vision. This indeed requires much more than the management. The teams which have absolute clarity on the purpose of the project, aligned with the vision, and have the autonomy to perform tasks, perform the job faster than the others. Hence while efforts are not directly yielding the results, a project leader needs much more than just measuring the efforts and reporting the progress of the project.

Don't get me wrong. I'm not saying that either managing a project is irrelevant for today's project. All the above factors evidence that 'management alone' is not adequate. We need much more than just managing projects. Is leadership an answer to this question?

Maybe, maybe not

Management is a subset of the leadership; the nexus of both of them creates remarkable results. In today's context, leading more and managing less is the recipe that creates a sustainable performance in the projects.

Factors that Reshaping the Project Ecosystem

Before getting any further, let us have a look at the factors that have reshaped the project ecosystem comparing to when the project management frameworks are laid out.

1.   **Increased level of chaos and complexity**: The element of unpredictability in projects is growing every day. Many of the tasks undertaken in projects are exploratory. Unlike in the past, where one had clarity and a fixed scope definition, today's projects call for greater agility, flexibility, and responsiveness to the development.

2.   **Projects are no longer insulated:** Projects no longer operate in an adiabatic environment, and seldom does a project can be carried out without the influence of

external factors. The project's viability changes during execution and the assumptions made about its feasibility are consistently challenged by factors such as rapid technology obsolesce, shift in the customer preferences, shorter product life cycle, new inventions, and competing products in the marketplace. Often, this might challenge the viability of the products, services, or results that a project aims to deliver—and these factors might even hasten the termination of a project. Hence, there is a greater need for responsiveness to external factors.

3.   **The shift in dependency**: Today, projects rely more on the human intellect, while most of the projects in the last century were primarily dependent on machines. The efficiency-focused methodology was well suited for those projects but does not guarantee a positive outcome for cognition-based projects that are driven by a knowledge workforce. The analytical framework for measuring the success or failures of projects also, unfortunately, disregards the inherent uncertainty and often accounts only for variability. This tends to stifle the creative process of projects and even acts as an impediment to unleashing the real potential of the creative process.

4.   **Projects are extensive and challenging to manage:** The intensity of projects is much deeper, and projects spanning more than a couple of years are being undertaken. An extraordinary level of complexities needs to be dealt with to complete projects successfully. Also, many aspects unfold as the project progress. Hence, sticking to the pre-determined arbitrary estimates, made during the initiation, is becoming less attainable.

5.   **Maintaining pace amid constant change and restructure:** Projects need to be agile and nimble, as the ecosystem at the time of completion of the project could be very different from the time it was initiated. The speed at which the right decisions are taken determines the success of a project—and a higher number, of course, corrections are needed during execution than what was necessary a decade back. The project team needs to be more agile and nimble in order to make adjustments to the project to sustain its viability when the product or services are delivered into the market. Requirements do not remain stable and swift response to the developments acts as a differentiating factor for winning with projects.

6.   **Evolution of types of projects:** Projects have transformed considerably from the military and industrial ages to the Information Age—from brick-and-mortar to radical innovation. The ratio of brick and motor projects to cognitive projects suggests that it is skewed towards the latter type. This includes the innovation drive, startups, and research and development projects to name a few. Projects in today's world require new skillsets, toolsets, and mindsets—hence, businesses have redefined the operating rules. Along with the general management and leadership methodologies, projects also have to adapt to a new set of standards to continue to be relevant and to contribute to today's economy.

7.   **Evolution of the intellectual workforce:** Today's project teams are more passionate about their profession and are considered as 'partners' in the business. There is a shift in the culture of the workforce. Skilled, obedient labor is a thing of the past—organizations now

look for out-of-the-box thinking and creativity. Intrapreneurs with complete ownership are needed to deliver the complex projects of today. Unleashing the maximum potential of human resources is the need here. Enabling environment, motivation, and sense of belonging are the requirements in today's ecosystem. A volunteer workforce also enables higher productivity, when compared to the subordinated laborers with carrot-and-stick methods of motivation.

> It is complex to conceive, difficult to plan, easy to delay, and much harder to recover.

Today's projects in the information era are more complex and vulnerable.

The changing role of project managers

The projects are considered as temporary endeavors, and hence maybe there is a much focus on the management-which gets the results done out of the given short time of these temporary endeavors. But nowadays projects have been an instrument for the organizations to grow, be it infrastructure creation, new product development, innovation, application development, or systemic improvement initiatives. Businesses achieve their vision through projects. I have been associated with projects for a long time, at the portfolio level they are continuous, yet each of the individual projects is a temporary endeavor. Project teams work for a longer part of their career in projects. Therefore, all the leadership needed for other domains is equally applicable to projects as well.

15

Consequently, there can be an increased level of leadership - management nexus to get the results with higher speed.

The fundamentals of textbook models, the book of knowledge like planning, organizing, executing, controlling, and closeout are still relevant, and that is the undercurrent that is needed in any project. Often success is not determined by following just the framework, success requires going that extra mile beyond what is prescribed in the textbooks. Project management skills like planning provide a foundational platform, but they need to possess more than just planning abilities. Some tools can upgrade an average project manager to the leader level. They need to be equipped with handling the intricacies that projects offer. A successful leader can influence the team to make decisions faster to align the team towards execution and to increase the value creation from the projects. Tools that are being provided here are targeting for embracing this need for the change to put the project managers in the driving seats.

Managing the length and leading the depth

Only three things happen naturally in organizations: friction, confusion, and underperformance. Everything else requires leadership.

- *Peter Drucker*

We need not take the view that project management is the opposite to project leadership. Project management can be an integral part of leadership. Both management and leadership are necessary to succeed in today's context. This viewpoint rises to a whole new paradigm of managing and leading the causes and effects of projects.

So far, the expectation from a project manager is to control cost time and to keep a watch on if there is a scope creep, which is probably the foundation level. But as the ecosystem changes and the role of the project manager also changes. Today's project manager is not only the champions of time, cost, and scope, but also leading the inherent processes that result in benefits like time, cost, and scope. Project leadership is like a tree - it has branches, leaves, flowers, and fruits, yet an important part is invisible which is the roots. The roots of the tree make the entire tree prosper and provide all the harvest it can.

"Project Management" is dealing with the results
"Project Leadership" is dealing with the causes that create the results
Together, management and leadership are essential in enduring success in projects.

17

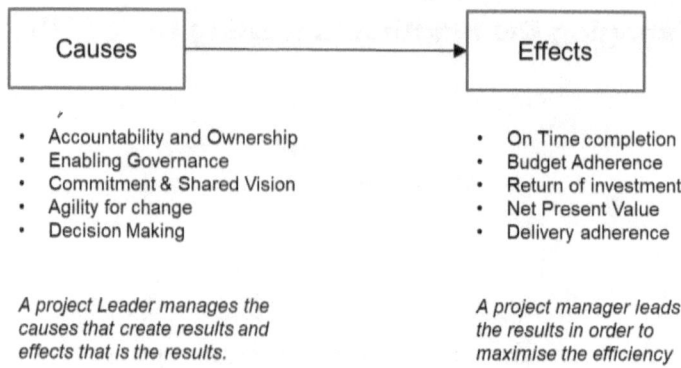

Figure 1: The Cause and Effect Focus

In projects, all the results which are being harnessed are essential as well as the causes which create those results. Dealing with those results, are management aspects of projects which ensure those are accomplished efficiently. Leading the causes, that produce the results is an approach to achieving project objectives effectively, we call this 'project leadership.' Analytical parameters like time, cost, and scope are the result, but the factors that produce these results are causes. 'Managing the results' required a different set of skills and 'managing causes' needed an altogether different set of skills. A project leader is the one who needs to have both of them to become successful.

The complete project leader is the one who is excelled in the delivery of the results as well as the causes that creates the results.

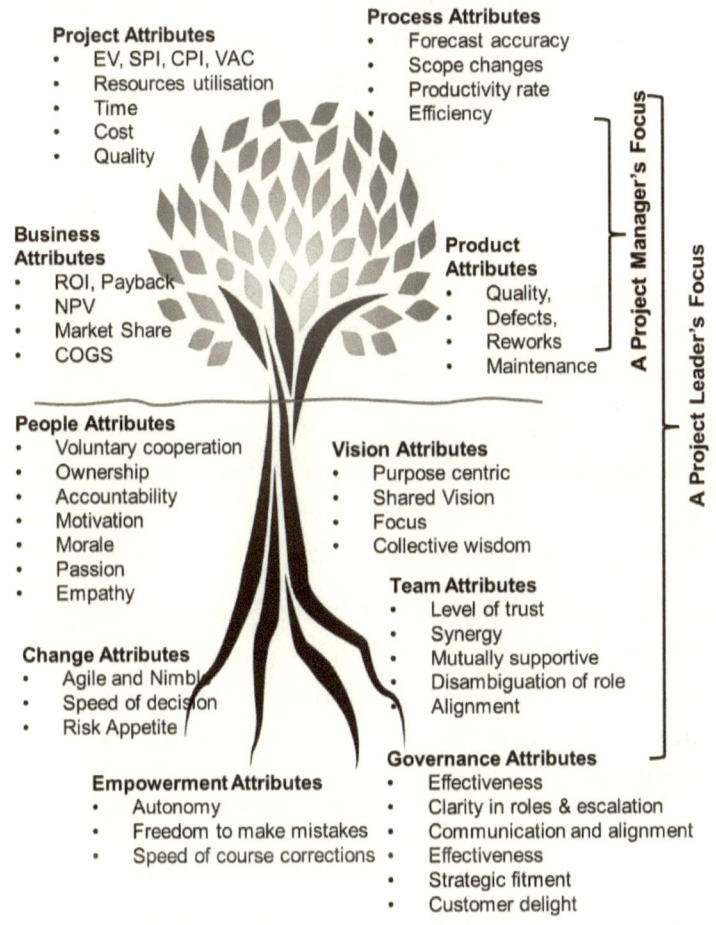

Project Attributes
- EV, SPI, CPI, VAC
- Resources utilisation
- Time
- Cost
- Quality

Process Attributes
- Forecast accuracy
- Scope changes
- Productivity rate
- Efficiency

Business Attributes
- ROI, Payback
- NPV
- Market Share
- COGS

Product Attributes
- Quality,
- Defects,
- Reworks
- Maintenance

A Project Manager's Focus

A Project Leader's Focus

People Attributes
- Voluntary cooperation
- Ownership
- Accountability
- Motivation
- Morale
- Passion
- Empathy

Vision Attributes
- Purpose centric
- Shared Vision
- Focus
- Collective wisdom

Team Attributes
- Level of trust
- Synergy
- Mutually supportive
- Disambiguation of role
- Alignment

Change Attributes
- Agile and Nimble
- Speed of decision
- Risk Appetite

Empowerment Attributes
- Autonomy
- Freedom to make mistakes
- Speed of course corrections

Governance Attributes
- Effectiveness
- Clarity in roles & escalation
- Communication and alignment
- Effectiveness
- Strategic fitment
- Customer delight

Figure 2: The tree of project leadership

Why Leadership?

It is very relevant for the project managers to transcend to a leadership role more than any time. It is necessitated by the three factors which have been discussed earlier.

a) The project as a workstream is continuous while projects are a series of temporary endeavors. Businesses retain the project workstream as project department or PMO, and these exist continuously in the company. These entities propel the growth engine of the organizations. Be its new product development, infrastructure creation, information technology, turnaround initiatives, modernization, even for the spin-off, the PMOs play a vital role and become an integral part of the organization. Hence unlike a temporary endeavor, which needs to be managed, the continuous entity needs to be led.

b) The success of the projects is determined by people and not machines. Machines need to be managed, but people need to be led. Business outcomes of today are determined by the people who are driving this.

c)Cause and effect are not directly proportional. When ideas become business, the ability to innovate makes all the difference. Hence the efficiency centric management combined with effectiveness centric leadership is what is needed to thrive in today's projects context

The above does not mean that the management is terrible. Project management remains an integral part of the way in which the results are ensured, yet the leadership is the one that gives the edge and sustainability of the results from each of the projects.

The toolset for peak project performance.

Nine tools are bundled together here, on consistent use, this has the potential to upgrade one to a role model for the project team.

You will be able to make course corrections in accordance with the intrinsic and extrinsic factors of projects and focus on the objective of the project. You will be able to be a change agent and foster the emerging culture, catalyst change initiative programs. While mastering these skills, you will be eventually able to progress report projects in a precise manner as well as focus on problem-solving.

Tool number **One**: Single Point of Accountability,

Tool Number **Two**: Two Pizza Rule is on effective meetings

Tool number **Three**: Triple opportunities is about unleashing opportunities that the 21st century has.

Tool number **Four**: Four ups is about making precise project progress reporting.

Tool number **Five**: Why-Five's, is about getting to the core in order to effectively problem solve

Tool number **Six**: Six Sigma in leading projects is about tiding the wave of the maturity model

Tool number **Seven**: Seven cardinal rules of project leadership

Tool number **Eight**: 'Eight or infinity?' is about co-holding the perspectives

Tool number **Nine**: Nine 90 Planning cycle is about systematic rolling wave planning

A **secret bonus tool** is a disillusionment effort.

With these tools, you will strive for mastery in each and every individual working on the project, as the focus of not on the quantum of work alone, but it is about unleashing the potential of the people. You will also be able to build a cohesive communication framework and bring the decision starvation to an end. You will be able to make your project being executed agile and nimble. This will make you bring people from versatile functions together in order to operate like a well-oiled machine. You will be able to kindle rigor in execution, make people accountable for tasks, and communicate seamlessly.

The Farewell to Personnel Managers – HRD Metaphor

Not long ago, but when the industrial era is fully occupied with machines, and when machines determine productivity, there was a workstream called 'Personnel Management.' The main focus of this workstream is to take care of the laborers and their welfare. This comprises time office, security, administration, attendance system, payroll processing, union agreements, and industrial relations. This was transactional and more prevalent in the industrial age – the focus there was machines and people supported the process by operating machines efficiently. The dominant skill needed from the workforce is the muscle power of the laborer who performed manufacturing jobs by operating the machines. The personnel management workstream was focusing more on compliance and with the labor laws, work efficiently in order to maximize productivity. The personal manager controlled the time precisely by keeping a close watch on when the labor enters the factory and when he leaves. They were also paid according to their attendance and overtime. Hence cost was controlled as well. The undercurrent motivational factors are based on carrot and stick; money was the primary motivation and punishment, such as loss of pay, unemployment as a fear factor.

But when there was a shift from the industrial age to the information age, there was a shift in the dominant factors that created results. In the information age, the dependence shifted from machines to human intelligence. Here the brainpower resulted in productivity, not the horsepower of the engines or muscle power of the human. This paved the way for the evolution of 'Human Resources Development,' which focuses on very different factors like motivation, knowledge, and skills development which target to develop the superior workforce in line with the organization's needs. In human resources development, the old practices which are no more relevant for the cognitive workforce faded away, the relevant ones got refined, and the new practices are added which enable the people to develop their skill sets, engage with the organization and contribute to the business. People are no more treated as laborers but as partners and associates. The function has becomes more of an indispensable strategic business partner of any organization. The HRD is now expanding its horizons and going that extra mile to keep the people motivated in order to achieve their individual goals as well as that of the organization. The carrot and stick motivation is no more relevant, the voluntary engagement and accountability are something that is targeted to make the business more productive. Nowadays, we can hardly find a personnel manager in organizations that is more transactional, but they have taken new avatars of various verticals called talent acquisition, organizational development, rewards management, training, and development, all in one umbrella of Human Resources Development workstream, which is a transformational role. The aim here is inclusive growth, the growth of people as well as organization. There is a book titled "Employees First, Customers Second: Turning Conventional Management Upside Down, by Vineet Nayar." I love this book for the title itself. What a profound message!

Story 1: Lisa is going to change the world

It was indeed not a desirable situation where she wanted to be. Yesterday the company just lost a 250-million-dollar opportunity. There are grim faces in the conference hall looking at each other. The team is customarily believed to be performing well in pressure situations and has delivered many time-specific projects earlier. But today is entirely different. Having been updated on this, their Chief Executive, took his chartered flight and he is on the way to the research center. It is better everyone has a good reason why the NCE-1 opportunity has been missed out.

FDA offers the first to file an opportunity to the generic companies which are developing cost-effective alternative generic medicine for branded products. To avail this, a company needs to start the product development well in advance and submit its dossier to FDA one year before the branded products exclusivity expires – this is called the NCE-1 date. There was a first file product for which recently they have missed the time of filing by just one day. And in the generic pharmaceutical industry, this one day makes a big difference. The product which she was trying to file is an oncology product that is believed to have the potential of 250 million dollars if it was registered on the first to file date. Filing on in NCE - 1 date provides 180 days exclusivity for the generic pharma companies to be in the market along with the innovator product. This means a lot to the business and shareholders. Now as the opportunity is missed out, this 250-million-dollar worth business will get reduced to 25 to 10 million dollars. Still, the company can make revenues from this product, but indeed it's a huge opportunity loss.

If they have missed out on this opportunity by months or even weeks, she would have been consoled. But they miss the bus in the margin of one day. ONE DAMN DAY!!!, which washed out 250 million dollars opportunity, she was unable to tolerate.

25

This is the story of Lisa May, who just assumed a leadership position in PMO of a leading generic pharmaceutical player. Her scope of work includes new product development, scaleup, launch, and commercialization. There are multiple departments indeed involved in this entire process, including research and development organization, global manufacturing organization, regulatory affairs, launch organization, and marketing. As you see from the description within the company, these are large entities, which have their ecosystem. They operate with their own priorities. Lisa and her team bring all of them together to keep the new product pipeline ticking.

Every product gets developed at their R&D center. Research and development are more involved in new product development, and the scientists are indeed hyperactive in such programs. So, he had fewer worries about this particular function. But the product developed need to be manufactured at factories that are already producing multiple commercial products. Here the global manufacturing organizations' priority would be finishing up their targets rather than disrupting that with an unestablished new product. New products when it is being manufactured at commercial facilities, there is a high chance of failure because those products are not yet established. Hence the manufacturing organization always has the reluctance to take up new products. Once these products are manufactured being pharmaceutical products, this needs to be registered with the regulatory agencies and approval needs to be sought to market this product. The regulatory affairs department is a different species altogether. They would expect all the documents to come to their desk to compile that and then file in the respective countries. Then it goes to the launch department for planning their launch on approval. Launch department as they hardly get any new products to the pipeline is a highly demotivated identity also over a period of time developed sluggishness.

Meeting with the CEO was chaotic, everyone had gone into a defensive mode and accusing others of the failure. Each department tried to cover their back and informed that they had done their work well, and this opportunity was missed because of other departments. The CEO did not like the scene but concluded that as individual groups even if they have performed well, collectively they failed. He wanted to speak to Lisa, as a head of PMO she might have been dispassionate about the individual departments, but be able to see the big picture

"We will have to hold these people responsible" she was in a complaining mode to the Chief executive.

"Why these guys are behaving like this, we need major shifts in the way in which we are working."

"We need to build the plants which are exclusively for new products so that you don't have conflicting priorities of commercial production and new product manufacturing."

"We need to have a more responsible regulatory affairs department; the job is not to move the document but take the initiative and ownership in order to file this product in the respective agencies."

"This zombie launch department needs to be dissolved, and I need to bring a lot of fresh blood into the organization, who will be able to bring a lot of energy into the launch and pipeline."

"The marketing office! Oops, they change their mind like anything. I understand market situations can change, but I don't want a marketing department to change projections they should figure out the way in which they can predict precisely the potential of every product and keep it the same until it is launched."

The CEO interrupted Lisa's allegations, "So, the bottom line is Lisa, you wanted to change the entire world. This May be possible, but it is a time-consuming process. Can I suggest an alternative which can start generating results instantaneously?"

"Yes. Indeed" Lisa answered,

"Instead of trying to change the world change yourself, instead of changing multiple other organizations in the company try to recalibrate the project management office, this is something which is in your circle of influence."

"While the world is not perfect, and there are many individual extremes an organization needed a change, the best way to start the journey is from within not from without. Be the change you want."

Part 2:

Foundational Principles

Foundational Principles

*Leadership is hard to define and good
leadership even harder. But if you can get
people to follow you to the ends of the earth,
you are a great leader. – Indra Nooyi*

Project management is something that we are familiar with, which is taught in several institutions and schools. Project leadership is relatively an emerging one, for this book, I was researching with various sparingly available literature. My submission here is that project leadership is something that cannot be defined but which needs to be experienced. The leadership has a very high bandwidth the leaders ranging from those who are focused on passion, the leaders who are focused on vision, the leaders who focused on the results, the leaders who focused on service, leaders who focused on values, the leader who focused on freedom. Every leader has the unique gravity that glued the followers to get inspired and follow them. Mohandas K Gandhi inspired the change of a nation from ruthless violence to non-violence, Martin Luther King made people share a vision of brotherhood, Nelson Mandela inspired a nation to embrace peace to gain freedom, and Abdul Kalam made the young population of a country dream about its future.

A formal definition of leadership fails to capture the true spirit of leadership with every leader indicated above. Attempting to defining the project leadership, in my opinion, is something that will lead to a very restrictive illustration. Instead of trying to define project leadership, I would seek you to focus on four foundational principles that enable leadership in a project environment. Project leadership is something that focuses on the following areas

- Purpose Centric
- People First
- Enabling Processes
- Voluntary Workforce

These are the four foundational aspects that a project manager needs to start focussing on to embark on her journey towards leadership. These are not in any way mandated by any institutes or standards. Yet these are something that the project leader herself has to imbibe to address the leadership lacuna in projects.

Purpose Centric

All things are created twice; first mentally;
then physically. The key to creativity is, to
begin with the end in mind, with a vision and
a blueprint of the desired result. - Stephen
Covey (Covey S. R., 2004)

Purpose centricity is the cornerstone of project leadership. These are two words, Purpose and Centricity. The purpose is the core value that is being created by virtue of the project, and the centricity is the directional orientation and alignment of the entire project that the team needs to have at any phase of the project.

Story 2: Jack Brown's and 'Eutopia App'

Organizations employ information technology systems and tools to support and enhance the ways their people work. The objective of creating these abilities is to facilitate and communicate, increase transparency within and between workstreams, enable more sensitive and sophisticated data analysis, and ultimately create an atmosphere in which managers can make timely and well-informed decisions. When Jack Brown assumed the highly challenging role of the company, Chief Technology Officer - CTO, he was equally intrigued by the opportunity given him to modernize the antiquated procedures and processes of the business.

One of the significant challenges Jack faced was to implement a state-of-the-art project management system that would transform the productivity of the company, increase the transparency of information, facilitate communication, improve action tracking and provide a collaborative platform for the project teams to work with. Jack evaluated several solutions and ultimately considered one of the leading enterprise project management software tools, called 'Eutopia.' This sophisticated software could not only publish the WBS to the team and enable the team members to update the system themselves online, but it also came equipped with a SharePoint for storing project data and documents. Besides, Eutopia provided a chat room capability where the teams could meet up virtually and collaborate. It had online project dashboards, as well as risk and issue registers with an advanced risk matrix able to classify each risk into various customizable categories in accordance with the risk priority number, also known as RPN.

Furthermore, the same software could run as an app on all smartphones and tablets in addition to laptop and desktop workstations. It seemed the only thing that this software couldn't do was make coffee, and Jack was sure that he had found the 'messiah' solution. Eutopia would be able to address multiple issues at once, and he was confident that this would immensely benefit the project teams and the company as a whole

Knowing the importance of effective implementation and deployment Jack appointed a dedicated team comprised of a top technical consultant and several internal associates, who spent over 6 months implementing the software based on industry standards. Eutopia would be all things to all people, move projects along in record time, and analyze trends to enable continual improvement of work processes. When the system went live, the implementation team was wildly enthusiastic, and Eutopia was off to a great start, thanks to an intelligent and colorful internal promotion campaign the consultant had designed and strong support from senior management. Numerous training sessions were organized to show the different kinds of users the wonders of Eutopia, and although attendance at the training sessions was sometimes sparse, and fell short of the 100%

participation target, Jack was confident that the on-site support team would be able to answer all questions and solve all problems.

However, post the grandeur 'go-live' session as people started working with the new system enthusiasm waned, and fewer people were using the chatroom and share point features than envisioned. Feedback from the users was discouraging as the team members realized that in addition to their already overloaded inboxes, they were getting numerous task reminder emails on a daily basis. Initially, some tried to update their pending tasks, but ultimately because of the cumbersome updating system, they chose to report the status directly to the project manager by picking up the phone to request that the project manager "do his job" and update the tasks in the enterprise system for them. After all, the system is a project management system, right? And project managers are responsible for maintaining the schedules up to date, aren't they? This, in turn, resulted in an unexpected increased workload for the already heavily-loaded project managers, who were starting to show signs of burnout. To improve efficiency and unclutter their inboxes, several team members realized they could divert the task alerts from Eutopia to a separate email folder (spam), preventing those alerts from "distracting" them from doing their "real" work!

The mobile phone app too turned out to be an utter disaster. The user experience was not as fun, friendly, or intuitive as other apps they used to like Google, Instagram, and Facebook. Jack's project leaders did not think it was fair to compare these "simple" search engine and social media "fun-ware" apps to a serious work application. Sure, Eutopia is way more complicated, but didn't it fulfill a critical purpose as well as provide crucial project data? How could task owners, managers, and other professionals compare the performance and ease of cloud-based social media to that of a powerful, sophisticated, and highly confidential PM system which depended on the company's own firewall, server, wi-fi, and bandwidth limitations? It seemed the more that Jack encouraged his team to give him creative and helpful solutions to the objections raised by the users, the more he received colorful and creative excuses for not being able to make the system any more user-friendly.

Jack quickly put together a task force to improve the performance of the enterprise system, but he feared that he would never regain the momentum or the initial enthusiasm now that it had stalled out in the execution. Worse, he was afraid that whatever grace and credit he was initially given when implementing the system for the first time was lost forever among those outside of his own team.

The following week Jack discussed this with his boss, the company CEO, Harry Nilsson, along with his plans to re-energize the organization. Through massive public relations within the company, he was going to ensure an increased rate of Eutopia adoption. He was planning promotional campaigns including Eutopia printed t-shirts, mousepads, special stylus-headed pens, and even competition with prizes for the top users.

"Jack, I think you're missing the point. The problem is not about t-shirts and prizes. Let's take a moment to get back to basics. First, you have to realize that an IT project should not start as an IT project" Harry said

"What do you mean?" Jack was puzzled

"Let me ask you a question when you start planning an IT project, where do you begin?"

"Technology, of course. We need to bring the latest and most advanced technology to the company; we want to beat the market with respect to technological excellence" Jack was proud of the direction in which he was steering the company.

"That is exactly the problem," answered Harry. "The way to begin an IT project is not from technology, but from the value that it provides to the customers, to fulfill their unmet needs. The IT projects in our company are not IT projects, per se, but rather business projects managed jointly by IT and the business unit that will benefit from it."

What do you think the most important objectives of any IT system are? asked Nilsson

"That's easy" replied Jack and continued, "every system needs to be able to solve those issues and challenges that our teams are telling us to make it too difficult, time-consuming, or resource-intensive to run an effective business process and make well informed and timely decisions."

"That's right on the money, Jack, but is that enough on its own. Remember, as Steve Jobs is often quoted as saying, 'People don't know what they want until you show it to them…our task is to read things that are not yet on the page.' That's why it is vital to add value beyond what was envisioned by the user, which we accomplish by familiarizing him with the further capabilities of the technology available. Such projects need to start with the customer. The first thing is to identify, understand, and define the issues we need to address before proposing any solution. It is also of key importance to ensure that the solution we provide is not more complex than the problem we initially set out to solve"

Confused, Jack said, "I'm not sure I'm getting you, don't we want the company to have the finest, cutting-edge technology?"

"Yes, indeed, we would like to have the best of the technology available, but that is not an objective in itself. First and foremost is the business requirement. When we are technology-driven, we tend to jump into solution mode before fully understanding the actual problem. If your technology does not solve the user's problem feasibly, they

simply won't use the technology no matter how advanced it is. In essence, you risk technology overload, like trying to swat a fly with a bus. Too many features to maintain without an effective and efficient solution to the problem you need to resolve. So, we shouldn't be surprised when our users don't adopt the solution offered. The software needs to serve the user, not the other way around. Don't let the tail wag the dog.

"Consider Google, for example, which is being compared with our Eutopia. Google addressed a basic user need simply and elegantly. Then, as features were added, they did not interfere with the basic functionality but built these more advanced capabilities around it. These newer solutions continue to address the remaining pain points of the customers and gradually add value by add-on applications, but never overcomplicate."

The discussion continued until Jack finally saw the light. He would continue to pursue technological excellence, but now he understood that the purpose of any IT initiative is to serve the business. Harry really gets it, he thought. Before becoming CEO, he was head of Sales and Marketing and continues to see his role as providing products to customers every single day. No one else in the company has his top-notch business acumen or his big-picture view of the entire industry and our place within it. It is no coincidence that he was appointed CEO of the whole organization. Learning the business from a businessman like Harry helped Jack to understand that his customer's purpose must always be his first priority, and meeting those needs be both the starting point for his initiatives and the goal of his efforts.

The purpose is something that the customer wants from the products, services, or results that a project aims to deliver. As Harvard professor Theodore Levitt says,

38

"People don't want to buy a quarter-inch drill,
they want a quarter-inch hole!" (Martin,
2009)

People buy products and services to fulfill a 'job to be done' or to achieve a goal. Similarly, each project is triggered by an ultimate purpose or value addition that is to be delivered to the customer. Accomplishing this purpose on time, with high quality, achieved within scope and cost are to be considered as a whole to determine if the project is successful or not. We call this the 'whole project paradigm.' The purpose becomes the nucleus of the project and defines the project's success or failure. Hence, establishing the core purpose clearly and demarcating it from additional benefits is critical. The core purpose can be delivered by undertaking various efforts. It is essential to understand that the efforts themselves are not projects—hence, identifying efforts and purpose and not mixing them up becomes equally important. The answer lies in two fundamental questions, 'what' and 'why' at the beginning of the project. And if you don't get that move on to the next question 'who,' the one can define the purpose of you. Now you can relate to how directly measuring the completion of tasks or WBS does not result in furthering a project.

The purpose of a project is to be identified without any bias, as this is the single most crucial factor in a project. One of the best ways to determine the purpose is to get the customer to define the core value that needs to be delivered through the project. This might be a new product or an answer to a question, a solution to a problem, a product that fulfills an unmet need, or proving or disproving a hypothesis. Understanding what the customer wants from the project is vital. It is not an easy task to define this, particularly in a novel product development process, as there is no precedence, as it is easy to misunderstand the attributes of the project as the purpose. If a customer is not able to define the value and comes up with an attribute to describe what she wanted, there are time-tested methodologies such as market research and new-age techniques such as Value Proposition Canvas (Yves Pigneur, 2015) that can be used to define the project's core purpose. The purpose becomes the nucleus around which all of the project's activities are built. A purposeless project is like sailing a ship without knowing the destination—it is better not to begin the journey without defining the goal upfront.

People First

"The P in PM is as much about 'people management' as it is about 'project management." - Cornelius Fichtner, PMP, CSM - PM Podcast

The most important resource of the project is people, not money or not even machines. Putting people first is one of the shifts in the project approach, which would get the ecosystem to move towards a more conducive environment. People are everything in projects, the customers, the project teams, the sponsor, and each and every stakeholder in a project.

The project is not being executed by 'perfect little robots,' but the people with limitations and constraints at the same time have tremendous potential to outperform the robots, given the right level of motivation and involvement. Hence the project needs to be people-centric in order to unleash the potential from them.

Today, projects rely more on the human intellect, while most of the projects in the last century were primarily dependent on machines. The efficiency-focused methodology was well suited for those projects but does not guarantee a positive outcome for cognition-based projects that are driven by a knowledge workforce. The analytical framework for

41

measuring the success or failures of projects also, unfortunately, disregards the inherent uncertainty and often accounts only for variability. This tends to stifle the creative process of projects and even acts as an impediment to unleashing the real potential of the creative process.

There are three significant ways in which project leaders can put people first,

- Making people successful
- Keeping the right people in the right place and ensuring the success of the project and
- Aligning the system and processes to people-focused

The paradigm shift of projects from the Industrial Age to Knowledge Era

Systems such as PERT or GANTT were initially developed for purposes that apply to industrial and military applications. These may not be entirely adaptable as such for projects that we are currently working on. In the Knowledge Era, several new factors will engage the workforce.

> *Our current business operating system—which is built around external, carrot-and-stick motivators—doesn't work and often does harm. We need an upgrade. And science shows the way. This new approach has three essential elements: 1. Autonomy – the desire to direct our own lives. 2. Mastery – the urge to get better and better at something that matters. 3. Purpose – the yearning to do what we do in the*

service of something larger than ourselves: (Pink D.
H., 2008)

Every shift in the human race—from hunter-gatherers to the information Age—has proven that productivity has increased significantly, by over a hundred times. In the Information Era, projects deliver value that is several times that of those in the Industrial Age. The use of techniques developed for Industrial-era projects undermines the capability of the knowledge worker to deliver according to expectations. In today's world, we don't call them 'workers' but 'associates' and 'partners.' These people are to be led rather than to be managed.

	Hunters and Gatherers	*Agricultural Age*	*Industrial Age*	*Information Age*
Workforce	Hunters and gatherers	Farmers	Factory workers	Knowledge workers
Skillset	Strength	Strength Tactics	Specialist Discipline	Intellect Creativity
Mindset	Survival of the fittest	Organized Community living, Patience.	Leadership and followership	Passion Volunteer ship DIY
Tools	Hunting tools	Farming Tools	Machines Systems Automation	Information Innovation Internet
Focus	The need of the hour	Independence	Efficiency Effectiveness	Purpose Value Creativity Interdependence
Motivation	Food Survival	Community living Being in control	Targets, Rewards Recognition Carrot-and-Stick	Equity Ownership Making a difference Shared Vision

Ecosystem	Individual Family	Family Community	Pyramid consist of laborers, employees, leaders, and business owners	Intrapreneurs Partners Associates

Figure 3: Project ecosystem of various ages

There is also the emergence of the Conceptual Age as indicated by Dan Pink in his book, 'A Whole New Mind: Why Right-Brainers Will Rule the Future' (Pink, 2006), which demonstrates that the creators and empathizers will rule the world, going forward.

Thomas Alva Edison is regarded as the pioneer of the first industrial research laboratory. What if Edison considered his making of the incandescent electric bulb as a 'project'? As per our project management practices, it would have been termed a failure and would have been closed long before he would have 'seen the light.' In today's context, several startups begin with a flexible framework and progressively elaborate over time. Take, for example, Facebook, when it was founded as a startup. If Mark Zuckerberg waited for a project charter with an accurate estimate of time, cost, and scope upfront, it would not have become what it is today. This approach allows the projects to unleash their potential and helps them reach the ultimate goal. However, the underlying need is to have a clear, unambiguous purpose, which will stand as the true north of the project.

Characteristics of an Information Era project

A project is progressively elaborated and needs to undertake many steps which are not visualized initially to accomplish its purpose. Also, there is seldom a direct link between cause and effect. Hence, trying to determine an accurate timeline becomes a challenging task.

An information era project has a more cognitive dependency. As human minds create a project in this era, the efficiency of a project is determined by how best human resources work and how motivated they are. Hence, a sense of ownership, a shared vision, and passion are needed. In the industrial age, well-oiled machines are required to perform effectively; in the information age, the human mind has to be enabled with ownership and involvement to perform the tasks better.

Finally, the external environment has a significant influence on the project feasibility and viability of the product and its lifespan. Hence, there is a need for a project management framework that addresses all these elements—a method that can enable rather than restrict.

People imperatives:

The following are some examples of imperatives that enable clarity of focus on people of the project

- People-centric policies and framework
- Offering flexibility and latitude to operate
- Creating a conducive environment that fosters innovation

- Enabling the power of ownership and mutual accountability
- Understand what motivates and aligning to that
- A culture that does not prohibits making mistakes
- Enable collaboration than competition
- Engage people on the project
- Creating a shared vision
- Making people part of the process
- Self-empowered teams
- Decentralized decision making
- Empowering people and hold them accountable
- Avoid restrictive process and encourage flexibility
- A culture that respects an individual's strengths and compensates for weaknesses
- A learning organization
- Space for experimentation
- Kindle creativity
- A conducive work environment that enhances productively
- Fostering teamwork
- Reinforcing interdependence
- Mutual trust

So, the question is, do the resources 'assigned' to the project, or they are 'committed' to the project? If people are assigned to the project, they would still do the job, but it will be merely a job. If they are committed, they have an intrinsic motivation that propels them towards attaining a passion or ambition that they own. Initially, it is not strange to have people assigned to the project, but in due course, by clarifying the purpose and making them a part of the broader vision, they share this vision with themselves and become committed to the process. This indeed would create surpassing results rather than just getting allocated as a part of the resource assignment.

Enabling Processes

Management is doing things right; leadership is doing the right things.- Peter Drucker

Processes are one more fundamental block of project leadership. There's no scarcity of the processes, particularly when it comes to project management. Numerous international standards, frameworks, schools of thought, and several rivalry methodologies evolved over a period of time. Following are some of the methodologies which are widely used

- PMI Standards
- Waterfall
- Agile
- Scrum
- Critical Chain Project Management
- Spiral Staircase Project Management
- Productivity Lazy Project Management
- Adaptive Project Management
- eXteme Project Management

The only question is, which works better and which creates results. If projects are unique, there can't be a single method that fits all of them. Sometimes the methodology is overwhelming to the extent of getting confused with being methods, frameworks, and standards. Any of this framework can be used as long as it produces results, enables speed and velocity. Some of the criteria for evaluating a project management methodology are as below.

- The process is to be enabling rather than restrictive

48

- Need to be in line with the vision and values of the business
- Need to be clear and unambiguous, enable decision making
- Nurture collaboration than competition

There are advantages with every single methodology which is being adopted in projects. Many times, project management processes tend to get a little bit restrictive and operate in the control paradigm. The new wave of thinking evidence that there is another paradigm is the 'opportunity paradigm' evolving. Here the approach is to bring the best out of the people and mostly applicable to the knowledge workers who are involved in information age projects where the effort is not directionally proportional to results. In the industrial age, the capacity is defined by machines, but in the information age, the capacity is limitless, like that of the power of the human brain. The 'release' orientation targets bringing the best out of today's complex, cognitive projects. It is not the efficiency that drives the outcomes, but the motivation that counts. This focuses on unleashing potential, which results in performance.

In today's information era, machines aid in the human's thinking process in the projects. Predominantly, the creative process or 'brain power' determines success. When it comes to cognitive work and brainpower, these are not to be controlled but need to be unleashed to get the maximum from them. Hence the 'opportunity paradigm' is more appropriate.

Moreover, in the industrial age, materials, be it raw materials, cement, steel, concrete are the critical ingredients of a project. These have gone through a process to create results. Today in the knowledge worker world, we use less material and more ideas to produce results. Consider the software products, there are insignificant raw materials used, the raw material here is the cognition of the knowledge workforce to deliver the results.

The problem is the use of the control paradigm for information age projects and the use of the opportunity paradigm for industrial age projects. The capacity of the machine cannot be expanded by motivation. Hence the control to maximize the output per input is appropriate for those. But the knowledge worker has the potential of creating extraordinary results given that she is connected to the purpose of the project, having autonomy and accountability.

The purpose needs to be aligned with the vision and values of the business

The purpose of the business, vision, and values need to be in line with the way in which the projects are carried out. Sometimes as a project is a temporary endeavor and being done only once, there might be situations that force to take an excursion, but this leads to the misalignment of the team which is working on the project. The methodologies which have been used to drive the business are to be in line with the vision and values of the company.

Processes need to be clear and unambiguous, enable decision making

The methodologies need to be very clear systematic and straightforward, which in turn allows that decision making. This is because today's projects are driven by multiple teams spread across the world. Having a nonhomogeneous philosophy of execution creates chaos and confusion. Harmony between the processes which are used, which is in line with the very rhythm of the project. Decisions are essential elements of the project, which are responsible for the success or failure of the project to meet its results. The speed of decisions, the agility of the team to make course corrections, in fact, determines the results. As projects are unique endeavors, you don't have the precedence before, there will be many instances where one doesn't have a standard operating procedure to refer to in order to resolve a problem. Every situation is new, and each and every decision is unique to progress the projects. Hence enabling this is a crucial factor for success. It should not happen that people don't know to whom they have to approach for taking a decision. Clearly laid out unambiguous processes, responsibility, and communication matrix are necessary.

Enable collaboration than competition

The project management processes need to enable collaboration rather than permitting competition between teams. The execution of a project has evolved to become a complicated, interdependent endeavor wherein multiple expert groups are engaged at every step of the project lifecycle. The modern workforce has developed into a specialized vertical, such as master builders or the 'one person does all' no more exists. Hence, the one who develops a product does not test it, and the one who tests the product does not release it. There are specialized verticals that have the required expertise to carry out the individual segments of a project. Complex cognitive projects encompass multiple roles, such as innovators, researchers, manufacturers, regulatory agencies, technology providers, service providers, and quality units. These groups are interdependent, and knowledge transfer between them is a vital aspect of a typical project. The risk profile, complexity, and pace of these individual segments differ, and cannot be treated the same way. The planning process needs to engage these domains at appropriate stages. Today's project is more like a relay race, where multiple teams participate in the race. Even in an athletic relay race, as stated by Jon Drummond (the 2012 Olympics relay coach for the United States), there are specialists for each of the legs. The first leg requires the most explosive runner; the second, a good long-distance runner; the third, a turn specialist; finally, the fourth, the fastest of the four. The speed of all four runners as individual athletes as well as teamwork at exchange zones while passing on the baton determines their success. As the project progresses, the baton is passed on to various work streams one after another, and there is a need to focus on every section of the project to increase the speed of work and meet the intended purpose. The speed of the overall project is determined by the speed of the individual steps of a project. As in a relay race, it is often the current step that determines the speed—not the one that was completed or the one that is coming up.

Process imperatives:

The following are some process imperatives that enable clarity in projects

- A process that respects human nature
- No hard and fast rule

- Agile and nimble that enables productivity
- Open and transparent processes
- Not to control but to enable
- Enable partnership
- Enable accountability
- Encourage Empathy

The power of Voluntary Workforce

"You can buy a man's time, you can buy a man's physical presence at a certain place, you can even buy a measured number of skilled muscular motions per hour or day. But you cannot buy enthusiasm, you cannot buy initiative, you cannot buy loyalty; you cannot buy the devotion of hearts, minds, and souls. You have to earn these things. ... It is ironic that....the most advanced people technically, mechanically, and industrially....should have waited until a comparatively recent period to inquire into the most promising single source of productivity: namely, the human will to work. It is hopeful, on the other hand, that the search is now underway."

— *Clarence Francis -* ***Chairman, General*** *Foods*

The voluntary engagement of the project resources is powerful and emanates the results faster and better compared to the forceful allocation of resources to the tasks. This is particularly true as the projects are more driven by human cognition than machines. When people are engaged in the process of execution of projects, connected to the purpose of the project, they develop trust and commitment in the process and get involved in the project.

Very recently, I had an opportunity to put together a team of volunteers, to organize an event. The event was very successful, and there is an immense involvement of the volunteers in making this event a success. These are the same colleagues who work on our projects, yet when they volunteer for an assignment, the ecosystem is altogether different comparing to the regular project work. The speed, morale, ownership, and involvement are tall, and it is a pleasure watching them accomplishing the tasks one after another.

I could not resist my temptation to think about what if our project teams consist of 'volunteers' instead of 'resources.' Sometimes, do we undermine the capability of human potential when we consider them as mere headcount or FTE in a project? Some of the noticeable differences between resources and volunteers from this experience are as below.

Resource (or FTE)	Volunteer
Says "It is her responsibility."	Says "She is doing this, I will still have it checked if she might need some help."
Power determined by layers and hierarchy	Everyone is equal, the level of empowerment is directly proportional to the level of involvement
Needs a leader and instruction	The self-lead team operates without micromanagement when the purpose is clear
Appointed leaders – static	Leaders emerge as per the need, and they alternate based on their expertise that suits to the occasion
Tasks assigned by other	Tasks are taken up by self
Job description, responsibility, RACI matrix	Loosely defined responsibility calls people to volunteer for every task
The project manager calls for the meetings	One volunteer says 'let us meet by 4.00 pm at the lobby,' and others agree
Project Manager need to remind and call people for the meetings	Volunteers are available ahead of time. Moreover, if they miss the meeting, they feel bad

People who are engaged in projects are the individuals who bring the required expertise to the project. They do not consider themselves as numbers such as FTEs. Treating them as mere headcount and allocating them to the task undermines their capability. This leads to a gap between the expectation and potential of individuals. The commitment of people can't be brought to the project by just assigning them to the tasks. There is a shift in the factors that motivate a knowledge workforce. Their first question today is 'what's in it for me,' in every assignment. They have the choice to opt between companies, within the company between workstreams, and within workstream their choice of project. Research conducted by Ernest O'boyle JR and Herman Aguinis shows that a high performer can be 400 percent more productive than an average performer (O'BOYLE JR. E. a., 2013). Likewise, in a project, a highly capable and inspired scientist or engineer can deliver much more in a given time by utilizing the same amount of resources for a given task. This is a tremendous possibility in projects. This can result in a paradigm shift in the speed and quality of projects. Hence, a process that cultivates human engagement is the need for tapping the talents and skills which the knowledge workforce possesses.

By the fundamental nature of the people, everyone in the organization is intrigued to get on board in a larger mission and be a part of the success story, given that there are a clear direction and accountability. The moment the vision is shared, they would say 'Hey, count me in' and start spinning the wheel to become a part of the success story. This brings a more considerable momentum in projects comparing to enforcing someone with detailed instructions on how it needs to be done and micromanaging them.

While project resources wanted to bring their expertise to the table, add value to the project in the process, they also would like to sharpen the saw and make them more knowledgeable than they were before. They would want to develop mastery in order to gain expertise in their chosen field. That also is the 'what's in it for me' factor.

Projects in a way are a creative process. Every project creates a product or result or service, and the creation cannot be a compulsive process. Creation is at its best when there is freedom of thought, freedom to operate, and freedom to decide. There is a need for a fun and conducive working environment, which encourages them to innovate and get glued to the creative process.

Following are some of the imperatives of making people get committed to the project by themselves

- Clarify the Purpose
- Inclusive process
- Support people to develop Mastery
- Fair, transparent processes
- Transparent Decision making
- Rewards and recognition than carrot and stick

Clarify the Purpose

Getting connected to the purpose of the project makes people travel towards the goal. A resource who is connected with the purpose is aligned with her thoughts and actions that create incredible results. There are several social movements one can remember in history which brought diverse people together when they are aligned with the purpose. A project too depends on the people who come from different backgrounds and cultures and value systems. Clarifying the goal is something that magnetizes each of these resources in order to march towards the single purpose of the project.

Inclusive process

Here is a parable that demonstrates the power of people's involvement at every step of the process. *Hundreds of workmen were engaged in various activities at a construction site. Intrigued by the massive scale of activities over there, a passerby was interested in getting to know what is happening. He approached and asked the workman whom he meets first, "What are you doing?" The man replied, "I work here, and my job is to remove dirt from the earth." He walked further and asked yet another workman the same question. That man replied, "Can't you see what am I doing? I am preparing the plaster, which is used for construction." The laborer moved on. The passerby spotted another busy worker and asked him, "Gentleman, what are you doing?" The worker replied with a smile, "We are building a temple—this is going to be a place of worship. Many men and women are going to come here to find peace and experience God." The one who is involved in the process of the project* can make a big difference. Wouldn't it be great if our project teams are made up of inspired, involved resources?

Develop Mastery

This is a most important 'what's in it for me' factor. While people wanted to be connected to the work, they also are also in need of developing expertise in their chosen field. There are two major kinds of mastery that people like to develop through projects, the first is in-depth knowledge in a particular area and the second is broad-based exposure. The first one is in thirst for getting involved in more intensive projects as she gets to evolve as a Subject Matter Expert. The second has a preference for being Jack of all trades, for them having more exposure to a variety of projects is essential. There are preferences to Design, Technical, Managerial, Problem-solving domains as per the individual's motive to work. The key is to identify people and put them in the appropriate place. Having the right people in the right place is like completing half of the work, as this connects the people and projects.

Fair, transparent processes

When people are treated with respect and value, they tend to become a part of the business as a family. This is particularly true in some of the eastern cultures. Fair treatment of the success and failure and a transparent workflow enables people to directly connect to the project and engage themselves accordingly. Nontransparent, secretive practices would induce the creation of silos. Favoritism of a project manager also would one way or other impact sections of the project, which eventually impacts the part of the project deliverables.

Transparent Decision making

One of the common pitfalls which hamper the velocity of the project is how decisions are made. The project ecosystem is different from that of operations, and hence, this needs a different mindset and toolsets to make timely decisions and allow the project to progress further. Many times project teams crave timely decisions; knock the wrong door until they find the right one to conclude on some issues. Following a bureaucratical process saps more energy than actually performing the task in order to sail the project in the right direction. There is inertia that develops due to the silos, which in turn impedes the implementation of the decisions.

While decentralizing the decision-making is a preferred option, this needs to be combined with the connectedness to the purpose. A definite decision-making matrix connecting to the criticality and importance can be a good starting point. This combined with a well-defined escalation process, ensures that the project is getting unstuck in case of an issue in any part of the project.

Rewards and recognition than carrot and stick

I read in a popular motivational book by Stephan Covey that humans do things for two reasons, one is for preventing pain, and the other is to gain pleasure. Relating this to people involved in projects, are they work for avoiding pain or to gain pleasure! An environment that is based on carrot and stick rules operates mostly on avoiding the pain system. People don't want to miss targets, miss milestones, and lose their incentives. Also, no one wants to drop the ball as the entire team is looking at them. Such ecosystems are primarily based on avoiding pain.

A project team that is well connected with the purpose of the project and has a shared vision and they are excited to be a part of the project. Such environments have respect for people, high trust, tolerance for error, the ability to learn from mistakes, and being interdependent and holding mutually accountable for success and failures.

Likewise, these teams inculcate a sense of partnership and gaining fulfillment by getting the tasks accomplished. The rewards and recognition to be designed in accordance with that accomplishment. These are achievement-centric programs that aid people to develop mastery, have a sense of fulfillment, and be energized by doing things for the projects. The WIFM – What's in it for me – is the one that needs to be addressed first, and that is the way the individual, business, project, and customer get benefitted.

People are usually more convinced by the reasons they discovered themselves than by those found by others. - Blaise Pascal

Part 3:

Triple Constraints to Triple Opportunities

> *The traditional measures of scope, time, and cost are essential but no longer sufficient in today's competitive environment. The ability of projects to deliver what they set out to do—the expected business benefits—is what organizations need. (PMI, 2018)*

There is an infamous parable by Seljuk Sufi mystic Nasiruddin Hodja, of a man searching for a key under a lamppost while he lost the key two blocks down the street. While asked, he replied that he could search better as it is bright under the lamp-post. We too cannot find the solution from elsewhere but from where we have lost. Let us start with the infamous iron triangle of the project which has been used for a while.

Story 3: Conditioning

Elephants are being domesticated and used for various purposes across Asia. You might have witnessed this if you live in or traveled to India. The funniest thing is these gigantic animals tied with the very feeble rope or chain to a peg. It would take a minute for the elephant to break that particular chain that is holding it from freedom. However, the elephant would never try to free itself. The elephant rider, a tiny boy, called 'mahout' rides on the elephant happily and makes sure that the elephant obeys the commands that he makes. I wonder why the mahout is always skinny or is it a relative comparison to the elephant and the boy rider! Elephants are one of the intelligent species in the animal kingdom, yet it is a wonder how it gets captivated and working under constraints, not realizing its own strength.

The background of this is fascinating, and that is a perfect example of programming or conditioning. Being a wildlife photographer, I know the fearsome force of a wild elephant. These elephants are either

65

born or captured from the wilderness at a very young age when they are weak. These are kept in captivity, and they are initially tied with a tree or a pole, with a heavy chain on their legs. Propelled by its natural instinct, the elephant initially tries hard to break itself free from the chain multiple times again and again. However, at one point in time, it realizes that the chain is unbreakable, and it gets programmed in the elephant's mind. At that very point it stops trying to break itself free, instead starts enjoying the payback it gets from performing its duties. That is the breaking point when it starts obeying the commands and getting a part of the domesticated elephant camp. Then it becomes easy for the elephant rider to train this for carrying wood stocks or lifting heavy material, for construction, or even in the temples as a part of the worshipping rituals. I have also seen elephants begging in the streets of Kerala. As days go on, a lot of things happen inside and around the elephant. The heavy chain would slowly get reduced to a very thin string or even a rope. The elephant also grows to sometimes become one of the biggest and strongest. The large male can weigh up to 4.5 tons in weight. Yet, having strongly programmed in the subconscious mind, the elephant would never try to break itself free. It keeps on obeying the commands of its commander happily accepting the tiny rewards the mahout provides. Elephants living in captivity without realizing their own strengths is a stunning demonstration of the power of programming.

Something radical needs to happen for the elephant to reprogram itself, in order to break itself free and utilize the full potential. In projects as well for a long time, the project management fraternity has been advocating and operating under a framework of constraints. The key objectives of a project are to complete within time, cost, and scope. We are being thought of triple constraints and operating the projects within this cost, time, and scope framework which has been followed to date while there has been quite a lot of changes in and the environment around projects.

Here are some examples of how projects are conceived, executed, and controlled in the past since the Gantt chart Developed by Henry Gantt (1861-1919). This makes us realize the paradigm shift in the way in which projects are performed today. Apollo Moon Mission, Hoover Dam Project, Grand Coulee Dam, Aswan High Dam in Egypt are the early examples of projects managed by proper scheduling technics. "PERT" was developed to simplify the planning and scheduling process of projects. It was developed for the U.S. Navy Special Projects Office in 1957 to support the U.S. Navy's Polaris nuclear submarine project. All these projects are either military applications or something which needs mechanical energy.

These day projects neither require much physical work from the resources nor the military disciple. In this free world, projects need the cognitive ability of the project teams to conceive, develop, and achieve organizational goals.

The Iron Triangle of project management

Project is a creative process that converts ideas into products and services. A project manager is the one who drives the projects towards the accomplishment of the objective. The triple constraints, famously known as the iron triangle of project management, have been in use since the mid-19th century. The triple constraints is an ingenious way of expressing the relationship between time, cost, and scope, one parameter cannot be altered without affecting the other. This is what we call a constraint mindset.

- The quality of work is determined by the time, cost, and scope defined upfront in a project.
- The project manager can trade-off between time cost and scope as the situation warrants.
- Changes in one constraint result in changes in others to compensate without impacting quality.

This was very much relevant for the brick and mortar, 20th-century projects, where cause and effect are directionally proportional.

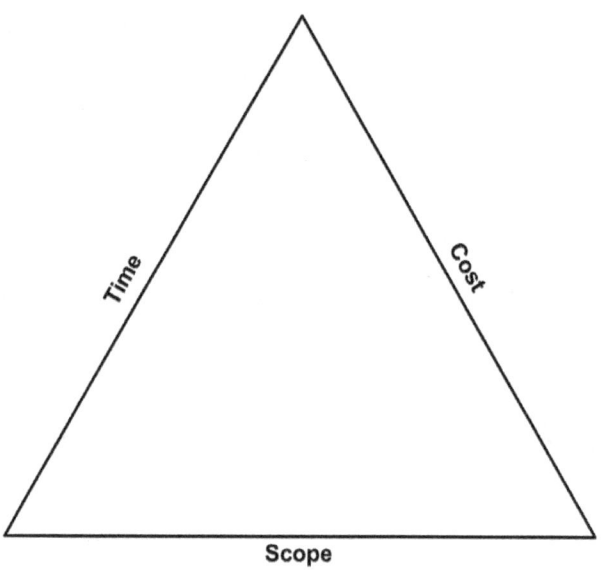

Figure 4: The Iron Triangle of Projects

Today, the only certainty is time, cost, and scope don't seem to be remaining as constant throughout the project life cycle. They tend to wax and wane throughout the project lifecycle due to their very nature and extrinsic and intrinsic factors. However, the dilemma is holding this as a measure of success based on an arbitrary estimate prepared upfront at the beginning of the project, assuming that it doesn't change.

Measurement drives behavior

As we realize, it was a strong belief that projects are to be controlled. Primary yardsticks of control are through time, cost, and resource utilization, and these are represented by schedule, budget, and project charter, respectively. Some of the yardsticks and drivers of the time in projects are

- Work break down structure
- Deadline completion date
- The right first time, every time
- Timesheets
- Crashing the schedules (why!)
- On track, overdue tasks
- Schedule performance index
- Slack, float, buffer

The elements of the cost measurement and control are

- Lowest Bid
- Cost control
- Cost escalation
- Labor Cost
- Present Value
- Cost at completion
- Earned Value
- Resource Usage
- Cost performance index

The traditional view of the scope is

- Features, functionality
- Scope creep in accordance with project charter
- Defects and reworks
- Scope change
- Change requests, amendments
- Baseline
- Arbitrary contingency

Earned value management was one of the best approaches to accomplish this in industrial-age projects. Sailing an S-curve becomes necessary in such cases. If measurement drives behavior, it is evident that when the team is measured against time, cost, and scope, they are motivated to control cost and time and to work within the given scope framework. Their desperation to meet these pre-determined parameters takes precedence over anything else, for that matter, even creative thinking!

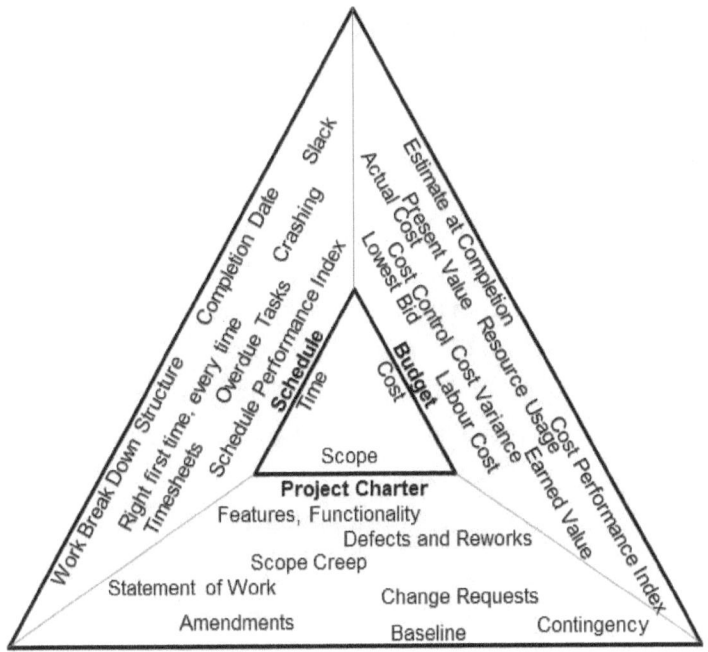

Figure 5: Yardsticks of the Triple constraints

What happens, in reality, is entirely different. As we have the predetermined arbitrary targets as the project success criteria, most of the projects are termed as failures in accordance with these targets at the end of it. Realizing this even the project management body of knowledge has moved away from triple constraints and moved on to a star model which consists of 6 parameters.

Scope

Scope: A client may not be poised to set the scope initially, but he or she may have a murky conception of something required to be done. If a project has such a starting point, then the scope is defined loosely and needs elaboration as the project advances. In fact, in some of my projects, I used to tell my people that the URS – User requirement specification stops only when the project is finished and handed over.

The changes will happen until there is no more time to change.

If scope creep is viewed as billing opportunities, many businesses banks on the scope change, eventually, this hurts the business-client relationship. Instead of opting for an arbitrary scope determination and complicated change controls, why not define the underlying purpose in the first place? The following are the eventualities by going with an upfront scope definitions

- Scope creep happens – murphy hits
- Customers discover new things
- Customer's preference changes
- The end-user has an experiential learning
- Upfront scope definition was not inclusive
- Translation errors in the scope document
- Requirements inadequately assessed
- Assumptions can go wrong
- Risks manifested
- No direct involvement of the end-user at the time of scope definition
- Progressively elaborated reveals new things
- Additional resource deployment
- Engagement of other experts
- Murphy strikes
- Additional work
- Added scope
- Subtracted work
- Quality factor
- Additional features functions results

- Progressively elaborated
- The seriousness effect at the delivery point
- Assumptions
- Features, additional, nice to haves.'
- Experiential learning of customer
- Reality factor - the gap between expectation and reality
- Technology obsolescence
- Variation in customer requirement

Time

There are several components of a project that is iterative in nature. There are various tasks for which duration can be determined upfront, and there are several others that need guesswork. The guesses are turned as assumptions and a series of assumptions are converted as project schedule. A software program crunches this schedule based on the software algorithm, and produces a pretty 'critical path.' There is an illusion that if the critical path is delivered, the project is in control, undermining the undercurrent guesswork behind these estimates.

Story 4: Richard Isaac's accurate estimate

This is the story of Rick, an experienced project manager who was assigned to take over and to save a failing project. Rick's objective was to complete the outfitting of a new auto assembly plant and ensure that the first cars roll off the assembly line as planned, 90 days hence. Management has been advised of delays to the project timeline, and Rick has been chosen personally by the CEO of the organization to bring the project in on time. Rick knows that he has just three months to start production and that every day of delay will cost the company

73

hundreds of thousands of dollars! The good news is that most of the equipment has arrived, and the installation and qualification work has already begun.

Rick confidently went to the project site as the PM and personal emissary of the CEO but also armed with the knowledge that the project was currently 32 days behind schedule representing many millions in cost overruns and lost revenues. While reviewing the current project schedule, Rick saw that it was a very high-level plan and that the estimated durations per task were long and unmanageable. Most of the tasks had estimates of 2 – 4 weeks, and even longer. From his long experience, he knew how hard it really was to estimate net durations accurately because people tended either to pad each activity with "reliability" time, or just the opposite, to be overconfident that they could get the work done in record time and that no surprises would arise to derail them. Rick was confident that if he could just add sufficient detail to each of these work packages, he could assign a realistic net duration to each activity and thus estimate the time required to complete the process. This detailing would help him to better understand the scope of each work package and recover lost time allowing the plant to start production within the targeted three months. He also knew, however, that under these circumstances, he would likely have to break his own long-held rule and spend a lot of extra PM time and effort micromanaging the progress.

Rick called a planning meeting and had the project team break up all of the large work packages into more detailed tasks. Then he had each activity leader reassess and to add new, more accurate estimates. The idea was to get back to basics, ignore any software limitations, and build the project flow using sticky notes on a huge wall, clearly noting which activity had to complete before another activity could begin. Once this was done, the PMs could then transfer the tasks to the software. Rick also insisted that the employees responsible for performing the tasks themselves be involved in this process in addition to their leaders, in order to estimate the time realistically required to complete each task. Finally, with this refined level of project detail, a more accurate estimate of the timeline could be calculated. This heightened level of task interdependence and visibility would also help to understand where the deployment of additional resources, or working on two or more activities in parallel could help in reducing the overall project duration, which was the ultimate goal.

After two seemingly endless days of rigorous planning sessions, gallons of coffee, countless pizzas, and lots of midnight oil burnt with the project managers and functional experts, the project managers fed the data in the project scheduling software to recalculate the project estimate. However, as Rick reviewed the calculations, he was devastated to find that his carefully prepared plan showed that in all probability, the plant startup date was actually delayed by a further 27 days.

This was astonishing, Rick was under the impression that the breakdown of larger activities into their component parts would result in bringing down the duration. Paradoxically, the teams which had committed to completing these general tasks in "a week's time" had been way overconfident. They found that the sum of the parts was actually greater than the whole and that once each package was broken down into manageable pieces, they actually needed a bit more than one week's time to complete that task. The reasons were many. Some durations were increased because the work was initially underestimated based on misplaced optimism. Another source of technical error was including weekends as available working days. Finally, some key activities had been missed out entirely, including the documentation that needed to be inspected before the plant could be approved to be opened. Yes, there were a few work packages where the durations were reduced as well, but this was not nearly adequate to recover all the time required. The reality was that once the plan was carefully and properly in place with all the relevant activities detailed, the plant was going to be delayed by a further 27 days. By this point, Rick wished that the project had been planned more prudently from the start. While the project manager within him felt satisfaction that he now had a good plan in place that was a reasonable estimate of the reality ahead, he also knew that he was going to have to communicate a very difficult and unpopular message back to the board.

The following are some of the on-ground realities which offer challenges while targeting to deliver an arbitrary estimate.

- Need for more time than envisaged
- Present bias
- Errors in estimation
- Time is fungible to the resources
- The probability of meeting the estimated initially timelines
- Student syndrome
- Parkinson's effect – work expands to the time available
- Bad multitasking
- Complicated work, unable to determine timeline precisely
- Failures rework
- Repeated iterations
- Stretched
- Additional iterations
- Sacred cow schedule estimates
- The probability of success on time
- Snowballing effect towards the end

Cost

If the time and scope cannot be predicted precisely, the pre-determined cost also will be inaccurate. If the initial cost calculation is misleading, the viability of the entire project is questionable. Following are some of the aspects that work against a deterministic cost estimate

- Cost escalation
- Improper evaluation
- Fluctuation and prices, like crude price, gold &oil price, the dollar value
- Inflation
- Currency rate changes,
- Additional features,
- Reworks cost more
- Reworks
- Scope creeps' costs
- Additional resources
- Risks manifest
- Efficiency issues
- Future needs
- Business need expands
- Anything that changes time and scope impacts cost

The undercurrent hypothesis of arbitrary estimates is that the tasks that beat the time and cost estimates would be counterbalanced by those that finish ahead of the timeline to eventually get balanced. In reality, while the overruns and delays are passed on, the advancements and savings are not. This leads to a strange formula

Time delays get passed on to subsequent stages

Time saved gets wasted before starting subsequent stages

Work expands to the available time and is often not delivered earlier than scheduled. Even in cases where early delivery is feasible, the downstream workstream is underprepared or waiting for another prerequisite to begin the task early.

Iron triangle or elastic triangle

Surgery is a good analogy of a real-world project. It is a broad category of invasive medical treatments for specific reasons. Every surgery is unique and has a definite start and end. If a surgeon were given projects with a fixed cost, time, and scope, and his key performance indicators were based on this, what would happen? In reality, many surgeries go beyond fixed models. A surgeon takes stock of the situation on hand and makes choices based on his (and his team's) wisdom. The only critical parameter is the purpose of the surgery—which is the patient's wellness.

There are numerous reasons why the upfront definition of cost, time, and scope does not work particularly in today's complex project environment expecting the assessment of these three parameters to be static and unchanged toward the end of the project only remains is a wish.

The iron triangle model promotes a trade-off between these three parameters or choosing between being faster or cheaper or better. That is no more a choice today. Today's project requires to be the quickest and cost-effective and high quality at the same time. The products or services which are developed in such a manner thrives in the market space. In the compromises in any one of the above, that might result in an unsuccessful product in the market space.

From desperation to inspiration: So the iron triangle needs to be flexible enough for today's projects. The rules which seem to be appropriate a century ago do no more apply to the projects of the day. We had a strict adherence to the work hours even two decades ago, but now we have flexible working hours, though have multiplied productivity. We don't need to operate in a constrained environment but unleash the opportunities the 21st century has to offer in projects by enabling creativity and latitude to work.

The challenge in the cognitive project is not limited to sailing the S-curve, but in surpassing the technology obsolesce and getting a notch ahead of the competition. Engaging the heads, hearts, and hands of the team and unleashing their talent is the right approach to achieve this. Project resources owning the project is a very good first step towards achieving this. The environment is made more conducive so that they have a sense of ownership and enthusiasm. Hence, intrapreneurs and volunteers are needed to carry out today's creative process in projects. The employees' mindset will bring in results, but superior results can be achieved only by inspired minds that are connected to a larger purpose. Businesses need to cultivate inspiration models in the interest of benefiting from the knowledge workforce of today while executing cognitive projects. Many aspects, such as mono-tasking and having a clear vision of the projects, are imperative in enhancing velocity, value, and purpose. The new approach, illustrated in subsequent chapters, tries to address this.

Consider the shifts that happened between the last century and the information age. Time, cost, and scope had to be adaptable. Laser-sharp focus on the ultimate purpose, having the customer in mind in every step could help businesses overcome project failures. While the clients want the project to be released on time, they care about how it adds value to their businesses or lives. Often, the project goes to a point of no return where the customer needs this project as a part of an important mission that is a vital ingredient of a strategy. Sometimes the client has already spent on the product or service and is patiently waiting for it. In such cases, when there is a deviation from the initially estimated scope, additional funds and time are endowed as long as the project can deliver the core purpose of the project. This is because the project can still achieve the inherent value, and it is still naturally available in the project.

There is another subtle transformation happening within the project management fraternity as well. As projects depend more on cognition, there is a need for leading more and managing less.

The dependency on man-material-machines has been shifted to people-innovation-ideas. The materialistic things can be managed, but people and ideas to be inspired and lead. There is a need for project managers to become project leaders.

Project managers of someone who consistently monitor the project in order to see that nothing wrong happens. But a leader is someone who focused on making good things happening to the project and people.

The command and control are being shifted to inspiration and enabling. Swing to the leadership side is the requirement for today's project, unlike any time.

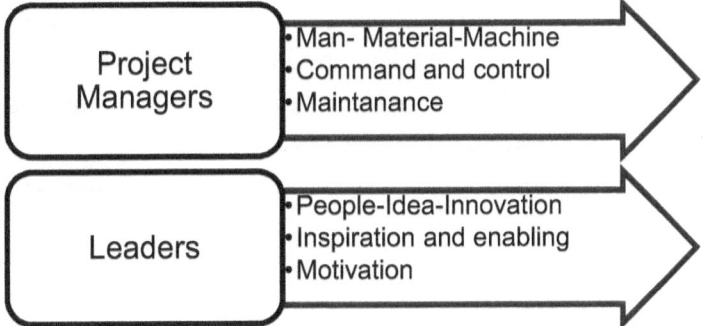

Figure 6: Focus of Manager and Leader

Transforming triple constraints to triple opportunities

The triple constraint is an intelligible algorithm to relate to the cost, time, and scope of a project that is still relevant for many projects where these aspects need to be controlled. Focusing on this gives varying degrees of success and merely depends on the accuracy of the upfront estimate of these three parameters at the beginning of the project. This triangle can be a handy tool for controlling an industrial age project. Traditional project management practices hover around the control of these parameters.

The entire analytical framework we have today is based on this trade-off. It is essential to have visibility of all these three parameters to use this algorithm effectively.

At the outset, for disruptive, radical innovation projects, where the upfront computation of these parameters is not viable, controlling this triangle is not feasible. Also, one can control only what is measured. If the accuracy of the measurement itself is under question, controlling the project based on this is counterintuitive. The triple constraints algorithm disregards the capabilities of the people who perform the project tasks. It assumes that a standard amount of time is required for delivering a scope of work by utilizing the estimated cost. This applies to machines, for intellectual work, we know that the output varies from person to person, based on eachone's inherent competency.

For today's projects, we need to see the different side of this triangle—we call it 'the opportunity side of the triangle.' The opportunity side has a slightly refined approach; this is possible by replacing the conventional measure of constraint with a new yardstick.

Dimension 1: Replace Time with Velocity
Dimension 2: Replace Cost with Value
Dimension 3: Replace Scope with Purpose
The logic of measuring time is to complete the project at the earliest. If the computation of a timeline is a problem for cognitive projects, the focus can be shifted to the speed of the progress of the project to finish at the earliest. The logic of cost control is to ensure that the project is completed within the optimum investment. The other side of cost control is to make sure that every penny spent on

82

the project is worthwhile, and create value for the client or sponsor. The logic of scope is to see that the project is aligned with the pre-determined objective in the interest of completing the project—the other dimension of achieving the same is to see it does not deviate from the project's purpose. There is tremendous potential for project teams to hone a new way of working by flipping the approach to improving each of these aspects rather than controlling them, mainly when there is the lion's share of unknown – unknowns persist in cognitive projects.

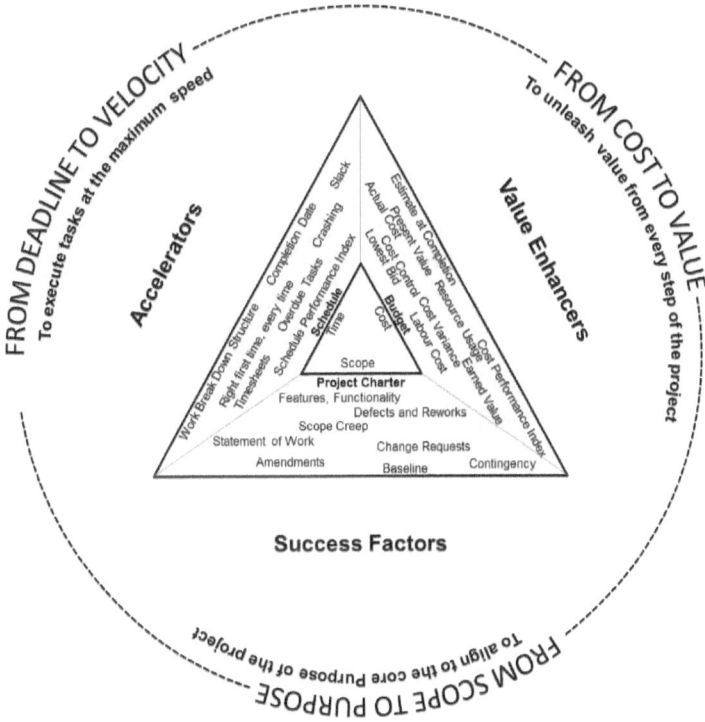

Figure 7: The Opportunity Triangle

Time: Transforming deadline to velocity

Traditional project management advocates a target date for project completion and the entire team to works towards this target. The larger project is broken down into pieces and all activities are organized in a logical sequence to derive the overall project duration. The project's success or failure depends on the team's ability to meet this target. Today, it is seldom easy to accurately ascertaining the timelines upfront. Hence, instead of controlling time, the focus needs to be shifted to increase the velocity of every step.

The underlying intent of measuring time is to see how fast the project can be executed, and products and services can be available in the market. To perform the task at the maximum speed and to get the products or services faster to the market to begin benefit realization. But ironically, it turns out to be deadline management, which stifles the creativity, that is needed the most in cognitive projects. The speed of an individual step determines the speed of the whole project, which determines the total duration of the project. This is like a relay race, where the speed of the individual runner who holds the baton determines the speed of the entire team. Increasing the velocity of every single step is an opportunity to reduce the overall timeline. This, in turn, results in faster delivery. This also has the edge over deterministic models as the time estimate for the activities itself is questionable.

Moreover, aspects such as Student Syndrome or Parkinson's Law can be preempted by focusing on improving the velocity of every step. (Student Syndrome refers to a tendency to procrastinate until the deadline of a project; Parkinson's Law states that the work expands to the available time.)

Is the approach here is instead of mastering the art of controlling time, switching to an increase in the velocity of the progress. The velocity of the project can be enhanced with a variety of **accelerators**, such as monotasking, decentralization, clear transparent processes, engaging subject matter experts, and reinforcing the collaboration between the teams.

Monotasking is one of the much-advocated methods starting from the critical chain project management framework, to have a focus on the task by each of the resources. The absence of distraction enhances the speed of execution of the one who carries out the project. Monotasking helps in avoiding the transition time due to juggling between multiple projects, reduces setup time, and promotes the knowledge curve.

Task mastery through constant single-tasking is another lever that can be used to boost the speed of execution. While monotasking and single-tasking are used synonymously, here we relate to them a bit differently. Monotasking is focusing and doing only one activity at any point in time. Whereas single-tasking is a task that a resource performs day-in and day-out repeatedly to gain mastery on that particular task. This is something similar to the discrete manufacturing which Henry Ford has introduced. A door fixer in a car manufacturing facility fixes the door day-in, day-out forever. That indeed allows him to gain mastery in the 'art of door fixing,' and he becomes the best person in the world when it comes to fixing the door to a car. Similarly, in projects, we have

85

people who can test, design, implement, project manage - when these people are allowed to do this, again and again, one after another then they gain mastery of doing such task. This is eventually enabling a reduction in several iterations as well.

Decentralization helps in gaining the velocity of execution. Empowering the functions which execute the project helps them to take a faster decision, be agile, and nimble to the development of the project, to reduce the complexity of communication. Decentralized project teams can benefit a lot in terms of having unambiguous directions. This, in turn, results in the improvement of the velocity of the project.

The **processes** in which the project team adapts to deliver their part of the project must be well defined. There are several ones once today available like a **full kitting checklist** to evaluate the readiness of a function to start their part before actually getting into the job. This avoids, later on, wandering around for some of the prerequisites. The stage-gate mechanism helps the transition of the project from one workstream to another seamlessly. This ensures that all upfront activities are complete and also clears the path for the downstream stakeholders to take the baton forward and execute the project with the fullest speed. The definition of turnaround timeline brings in a lot of visibility in the entire system as people know when they receive what they receive.

Seamless **collaboration** between various functions that take part in project execution is a vital enabler of the velocity of the project. Improved integration between workstreams to reinforce interdependency. Clear decisions that enable the advancement of the project without interruptions

Cost: Controlling cost to maximizing the value

In the deterministic model, the cost of the project is derived by summing up the costs of all individual tasks, materials, men, machines, and the methods needed to deliver each activity successfully. Today, cost estimates calculated upfront are seldom accurate. This is not only because of unpredictability but also due to the number of iterations that have to be tried to deliver a step. The lack of correlation between cause and effect also makes it difficult to predict the cost. The subtle intent of measuring cost in triple constraints is to create value from every dollar spent in the project, not the reduction of cost. If cost reduction is the only target, the project itself won't be needed as every project comes with investment! The objective of the cost side of the triangle is not to make a cheap product. Instead, it is indeed making the **value enrichment** in projects which is to be delivered to the customer. The dictionary definition of 'value' is *the worth of all the benefits and rights arising from ownership*. This can be accomplished in two ways: First, by providing quality of the products or services; second, by improving the utility of the products or services.

Our approach here is instead of controlling cost, maximizing the value through each step of the process and eliminate reworks, and obtaining cost leadership. There are several **value enhancers** we might leverage to accomplish this. Instead of deliberately doing something to add value, sometimes not doing gold plating or discontinuing unviable projects itself will result in value maximization. There are additional opportunities to obtain cost leadership by proactive identification and elimination of risks and reworks. The objective here is not to compromise on the quality of the product but to deliver the project with the right quality through value maximization.

Maximize the value of each step, must start with the clarity on what is **'nice to have'** and what is **'must-have'**. Once this is defined, it becomes easy for the teams to focus on the core purpose and deliver the same. Sometimes project teams end up in **gold plating** of the deliveries, which means refining and deliveries unnecessarily more than what is needed. This is to be avoided.

There are several opportunities today available for project teams to obtain **cost leadership**. This includes the use of **technology** to improve precision and efficiency, elimination of obsolescence; use of the latest materials, methods, and knowledge. Several tasks that could be done by a human can be performed by high precision equipment, with the utmost quality and reduced defects. Not necessarily this equipment to be capitalized every time, but can also be outsourced project to project basis.

The other side of cost leadership is to look at the **unwanted steps** and to pre-empt those. If there is proper value analysis done on the project methodologies and practices in a company, to your surprise it might reveal that there are several aspects, which don't align with the **core purpose delivery**, which consumes additional resources and consume time in the projects. Recognizing this and removing this from the process improves cost leadership.

The third aspect is to **add value** to the product or services in each step of the project. This starts by aligning to the core purpose, differentiating the core purpose to the additional benefits, and performing the value-added activities with utmost efficiency. Improving the quality of delivery at every step, which enhances the quality of the project as a whole. Many times businesses suffer from unviable projects, and they identify this at the late stage, already resources and money have been utilized, which is irrecoverable. Taking cognizance of this and **pruning the failing projects** in a portfolio early enough, helps businesses to employ their cost and resources only on the project, which is profitable. Failing early is better than failing later.

Advancements in the risk management domain help teams to identify the problems early enough. There are powerful tools such as **pre-mortem** to identify risks and to manage them effectively. This also helps in eliminating or minimizing the reworks, which might be required in projects. Reworks are the result of poor planning. Hence adequate forecast of risk through tools like pre-mortem would help in enhancing the value. In the research and development projects, the reworks until the final iteration are not going to add value to the product or services. Hence a thoroughly thought out plan to minimize the number of iterations is something that adds value to the entire project also passes on the value to the customer.

The use of **economies of scale** to reduce cost, **outsourcing** several aspects of the projects could not only use the expertise available elsewhere but also get these aspects cost-effective and faster. The use of **cloud**

computing is the best example of this. Also, the use of the **'subject matter experts'** pools available outside the organization to add value to the projects.

One of the best expressions I have learned about cost optimization is: *"Today's project teams have a lot of money to spend but none to waste."* This is a profound message— we must invest every dollar in the project tasks that result in the progress of the project and, ultimately, in the improvement of value for the customer.

Scope: Rigid scope definition to purpose alignment

In deterministic models, the scope is worked out by adding all that is necessary to deliver the project based on the upfront estimate. In cases of ambiguity, the scope of work is referred to ascertain what is in-scope and out-of-scope. The list of assumptions, risks, and workaround options is also worked out upfront. The scope also specifies who will have to bear the cost in case of a deviation. Quite often, in a typical project scope statement, risk manifestations are assumed to be covered by the customer. To avoid scope creep, everything needs to go right the first time itself. If any unanticipated tasks are to be done, it is charged to the customer. In a research project, seldom does everything go right the first time. When things do not go as expected, scope creep and change management come into play. All this, in turn, reduces the speed of the project and results in cumbersome ad-hoc decisions, approval, and paperwork. In other words, an arbitrary scope definition is not prepared for doing all that is needed to achieve the purpose but for all that is perceived as necessary in the initial stage.

Preparation for unplanned tasks, handling the unfolding possibilities, and responding to these developments on time is a critical differentiator in today's world. Hence, instead of holding on to a pre-determined scope, focusing on the purpose is the shift that is needed for cognitive projects. A laser-sharp focus on the objectives will help the team remain adaptable and responsible for delivering the same. Even traditionally, this was achieved through scope creep at the end of the day—hence, being prepared for this helps avoids going through bureaucratic change control processes that slow down the project's pace.

The core purpose behind measuring scope is to ensure that the intended product or services the customer wanted are delivered in full as per the original promise. But there is a time lag. This time span didn't matter twenty years before. But today in the fast-paced world, the time span means a lot with respect to customer needs, competition, technology obsolescence. Many times you will find the scope gets wholly changed from the time the project was initiated and when it is delivered.

> *How do you define the success of a project? Is it completing on time, below the budget, or delivering the pre-determined scope? In today's context, merely meeting the parameter does not guarantee the success of the project until this fulfills the very purpose of the project. Achieving the purpose and at the same time within time, cost and scope makes much sense.*

When it comes to purpose, it is essential to realize the real customer of the product or services. The sponsor and the customer could be different in many cases. The customer is the one who uses the products or services which is created through the project. A sponsor is the one who invests in a project and providing guidance to deliver the projects. It's key to identify the customer first in place.

The customer must be the best person to define the purpose of the project more than anyone else. If a project lacks the **customer's voice**, the product or services it creates not necessarily be successful in the marketplace.

While the customer defines the purpose, the alignment of the team that executes the project towards this is critical in achieving this. We call this **true north orientation.** The purpose is the true north and the systems, procedures, people; resources are to be working towards this true north. Remember you are only loyal to the project not to anyone else.

The process which is used to march toward the true north is bound to be a **change tolerant** process. This is particularly important in this age due to the shorter product lifecycle, technology obsolesce, fierce competition, and high complexity. The agility to tide over the obstacles and ever influenced product requirements determined the success and failure of the product.

To cope up with that, the process also needs to be able to **harness the creativity** of the people who are involved in that. More often there is out of box thinking required to solve complex problems which projects have to offer today than any other decade.

Customer's voice: The customer is the one who is going to use the product or services. As long as the product does not meet the requirements, it may not survive in the market, with an exception to the monopoly and regulations. Today's open market environment seldom offers the choice to be a monopoly in any line of business. Hence the project needs to be customer-centric, focusing on the need of the customer anytime. Having customers defining the scope and expecting them to be a part of the testing may not be possible, yet the following are some of the parts of the customer's voice at various stages of the project

- Original scope definition
- Purpose of the product or services
- Intermittent reviews and stage gates
- Demarcation of 'must-haves' and 'nice-to-haves.'

- Validating assumptions
- Testing and acceptance of the product

Customer inputs can sometimes surprisingly solve a complex problem that the project teams baffle within the group while handling issues. Hence engaging customers in the journey of the project not only benefits customers, but it also does for projects as well.

PROJECT VISION BOARD

One of these simple yet powerful ways in which the customer's voice exists in the project is to make the purpose of the project interwoven with the vision board of the projects. The vision becomes inseparable from the individual's alignments in executing the project as a shared vision with all stakeholders who influence the project's success. Taking feedback from the customers at regular intervals on various stage gates and review mechanisms ensures the customer's voice is a dominant propelling force of a project.

Your brain will work tirelessly to achieve the statements you give your subconscious mind. And when those statements are the affirmations and images of your goals, you are destined to achieve them! - Jack Canfield

Conventionally, once the project is identified, we get into the planning mode. But one key element which is missing in this process is to make the objective clear and making this a shared vision of the people involved in the project.

Getting into a planning mode immediately after the project initiation would be a little premature. Hence creating the project vision is essential. This has been recognized in various Agile models as well.

Vision board is a tool in which the purpose of the project can be clearly laid out, and more importantly, it is to be worked out by the team which is responsible for delivering the project. Vision boards are a more powerful visualization technic that converts the project objectives to the subconscious mind of the people who are executing this. The aim is not to add one more document into already overburdened project documentation. Creating a vision board can be as much as fun as it can. There are several ways in which the vision board can be accomplished, but one of the major prerequisites for this is to have many of the execution stakeholders involved in this process. Here are some of the several ways in which a vision board can be created.

a.   Mind mapping

b.   Brainstorming session with the key stakeholders with post Its, flipcharts

c.   A pin-up board in your office where you can pin pictures and printed statements.

d.   Vision Board computer applications or mobile apps

e.   Agile Vision Boards

My favorite process is to create a mind mapping. Mind mapping is a tool that is devised by Tony Buzan, and this is very much applicable for creating a project. One of my author-friend, Maneesh Dutt has written a book with the title "Mind Maps for Effective Project Management." This is a useful reference for the application of mind mapping into projects. Here is an example of a simple project vision board.

Project Vision Board

Purpose : *Why This project Exist*	
Customer: *Who is the actual customer of the project*	**Product/Service/Results Attributes:** *What really the customer want (get to the core)*
Business Goals : *What is financial, technical, strategic, capacity, competitive advantages of the business to undertake this projects*	**External Factors :** *Competitors, regulations, customer, technology-obsolescence that affect the project*
Milestones and Showstoppers *Delivery 1:* *Delivery 2:* *Delivery 3:* *Risk 1:* *Risk 2:* *Risk 3:*	**Key Constraints:** *Drop dead date, Expertise, Financial Spent, Resources Limitations with which the project team need to work with*

Figure 8: Project Vision Board

Following are some other important steps to create a vision board

1.   Get people to know the purpose of the project unambiguously

2.   Define clearly the customer needs and the value addition which the product the service is going to make- this is going to be the overarching need for every workstream to refer to in future phase of the project and would help in ease of decision making

3.   Get to know the people who are involved in the product including customers sponsors and other stakeholders

4.   Define the business objectives and WIIFM 'what's in it for me' for each of the team which are involved in executing the project

5.   Define how it is going to be achieved

6.   Start weaving all these things together in the way of a vision board. Be sure to include positive affirmations, energetic statements which can kindle the excitement whenever someone looks at it

7.   Make it visual - add photographs, charts, comments, pictures of the team members, numbers ($ and date), pictures of the customers. The more visual it is, the more connected it becomes

8.   Extend the project vision board to individual workstreams that they can add their contribution to the project. Leaves some space in the vision board for people to add their passion.

The idea here is to convert the uninspiring scope statement into an inspiring, well-connected vision board that people can relate their role towards a larger purpose. This vision board can be kept in the project corporate office and also can be kept in individual workstreams where people can extend that further to their part of the work.

TRUE NORTH ORIENTATION

The purpose of the project is the true north of the project. Period. Every effort, system, process, policies must be aligned towards achieving the core purpose. The purpose is the core benefit that a customer wants from a project or product or service. Everything else is an ancillary benefit that falls in the 'nice-to-have' category.

The purpose definition to get to the very bottom of the requirement from the customer. The scope, decisions, and approach from the entire team are going to be aligned towards this. Once the core purpose is defined, the timelines, decisions, course corrections need to be taken in line with that. Fostering purpose-centric project ecosystems is an essential first step towards the attainment of true north orientation.

Progressive planning is a needed process in sailing through the true north. It's like making those finer adjustments as per weather while having a good upfront plan of journey worked out. The rolling wave planning is the one that is useful compared to the arbitrary initial schedule. The reality cannot be planned upfront but can be handled with adaptive planning.

The team needs to be prepared to be agile and nimble to developments. The bottom line is that the processes need to be **change tolerant** processes. The complicated scope change control processes, endless documentation to conclude on the scope creep do not serve the purpose of today's projects. In reality, this documentation leads to finding a victim or to explore an additional billing opportunity. Either way, it plays a spoilsport in the client–business relationship. Hence **uncomplicated the scope change process**. Instead, a master plan and a high-level budget can be worked out, and the same can get refined by way of adaptive planning to deliver the purpose of the project.

Harnessing the creative energy is needed as the people are the most critical factors in a creative process. The agile and nimble actions to adjust to the intricacies, problem-solving requires much of this creativity. Leveraging **eureka moments** pumps up the energy of the resources which are involved in the project. Having a bench strength helps in adaptive planning as additional resources might be needed in the case. Letting people develop excellence is a dire need of today, and this enables the development of a center of excellence within the business. This would not be possible if the processes are not people-centered.

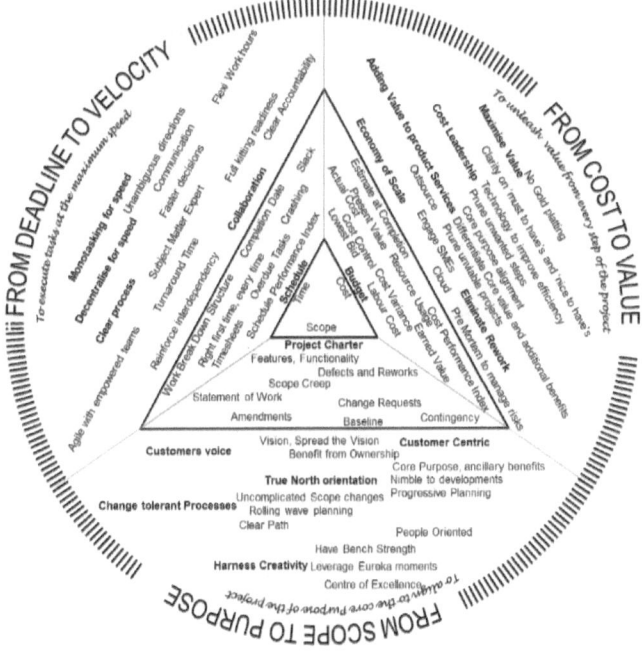

Figure 9: Yardsticks of the Opportunity Triangle

Three fundamental shifts organizations must undertake to get to the new paradigm

CREATE A SHARED VISION

The objectives of the project need to get to the core purpose of the project on why the customer wanted the project first in place. An unambiguous objective of the project becomes the single most priority of the entire project team. Time to be spent to define the purpose of the project vividly, mostly connected with the customer and not by the project team.

Making this a shared objective, as a true north is the one that helps to create velocity, align people towards purpose, and make the process cost-efficient at the same time. The Vision board is a much useful technic to be adapted to inculcate this.

REHUMANIZE PROCESSES

Decentralization, making the workstreams accountable for their tasks empowers them. Stage-gate is a useful tool in which this can be achieved. While the workstreams are empowered to make their decision in line with project objectives, the checks and balances are provided based on the stage-gate reviews, and course corrections can be made.

ADAPTIVE PROJECT MANAGEMENT

Rigid deterministic models helped the industrial era projects to progress. In the twenty-first century, the more adaptive the governance is, the better for the project. The entire agile movement is about this. The Information Technology industry fully embraced this concept and reaping benefits from it. But for other industries as well, where cause and effect do not have a direct correlation, this would be much beneficial.

So, we have turned around the triple constraints' triple opportunities. Is it the end of the story?

Not Yet

The Project Leader's Diamond

While Velocity, Purpose, and Value provide a new dimension of the re-casted opportunity triangle of projects, the triangle remains incomplete. Two elements are missing in this and which have to be the undercurrent while executing the project. These are 'customers' and 'people.' Any process in today's environment if it is not customer-oriented or people-centric it is not worthwhile to pursue. Add the people dimension and customer dimension to this to make a new possibility in the triple opportunities triangle. This results in a new paradigm called the **'Project Leader's Diamond'** which has five sides representing velocity, value, purpose, people, and customer. If a project team is oriented on these five aspects at any point in time, the project would be successful. The inputs, processes, and output of today's projects need to be oriented towards these five factors. Hovering all the 'measures of success' around these parameters will ensure that they can bring out the value and turbocharge the execution and ultimately result in achieving the whole purpose of the project. At the same time, the project is compatible with the customer's requirements and conducive to the project teams.

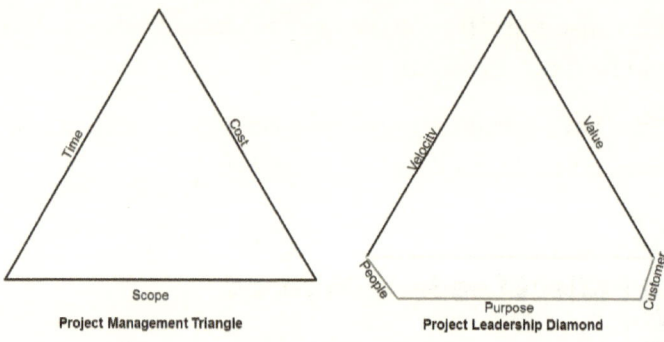

Figure 10: The Project Leadership Diamond

While project management focuses on getting things done by controlling time, cost, and scope, the new project leadership approach is to get the people first to achieve business goals. Richard Branson's infamous quote is

> *"Clients do not come first. Employees come first. If you take care of your employees, they will take care of the clients."*

Projects are not exceptions to this, by putting people first the Purpose, Velocity and Value would get imbibed in every subprocess and thus become an inherent strength of project governance.

The Leadership Dilemma: Hurdles in Leadership Deployment in Projects

Projects conventionally seen as temporary endeavors, since there has been a super focus on the completion of that within time, cost, and scope. The focus is overemphasized on these deliverables, and we can understand the reason, as people are engaged for a short while in the project until completion. The leadership practices are not seen as relevant, for projects which are temporary in nature. Leadership practices are seen as more relevant for enduring endeavors. Projects are efforts for immediate profitability. Indeed this is a very reason for the adaption of efficiency-based managerial approaches in projects. Several of the project 'management' standards are evidence of this efficiency centricity.

Nowadays, while projects are still seen as temporary endeavors, the people engage in the projects are being in the profession for a whole lifetime. Projects are the key growth initiatives of any business to sustain and thrive in the fiercely competitive market space. Hence project teams are perpetually engaged in organizations to create new products, services, or markets. Dealing with such as a part of the business is the first point of realization to progress to a paradigm shift in the discipline.

> *Projects may be temporary endeavors, but project teams are continuous.*

We have been doing this way;

Even some of the project professionals feel out of the comfort zone when challenged on the conventional wisdom of the control paradigm of projects. It has been done in this way for ages. Which indeed produced results and hence, there is no need to change. When ain't broke, why fix?

Not a mainstream process

Projects are not something that is considered as a mainstream process such as Operations or Marketing. But projects are still growth engine of any organization to expand to new territories to launch new products to maintain a life cycle of a product and to create a new capacity

The shift from an efficiency mindset to leadership

This means enduring a change, which is not comfortable at first instance. This needs people to go beyond the carrot and stick, an input-output formula that will produce instantaneous results. The leadership ecosystem needs to focus on the effectiveness

Long-term, short-term, and immediate benefits

Management practices are the one can have benefits demonstrated immediately. But leadership requires persistence, and it's about creating a conducive environment for people to unleash their talents. There is a lag time between implementation and results. Management is like harvesting wheat where income would be available within months, but leadership is like growing a tree. From the time of planting a seed, this requires years together for the sapling to grow and yield fruits. If one waits for that long enough, the tree takes care of itself, and you had to do very little maintenance. It creates an ecosystem by itself, which includes the birds, and the lovely creatures live in. In a project environment, it's seldom easy for one to decide for a long wait to harvest the benefits.

Story 5: The lost balloonist

You might have probably heard about the story of a person who lost his direction in a hot air balloon and asked one on the ground for help to figure out where is he. And then the person on the ground replies

to him with the details of the latitude, longitude, wind speed, and the direction he is traveling towards. After hearing all these details, the person in the hot air balloon replied that "are you a project manager?", the person on the ground replied "Yes indeed, how did you figure out?",

He replied that "You have provided so much data to me, but it doesn't help me to figure out where am I and where am I going towards"

A person on the ground replied, "By the way are you a marketing executive"?

"Yes, indeed, How did you figure out?"

"Because you are completely lost, you don't know where you are going towards, but you could find a person to be blamed for it."

While this is classical humor about project management as well as marketing, the matter the fact is that we have overwhelming data, analytics, and tools, sometimes it becomes too much that fogs the vision of the very purpose of the project. The KPI, matrices, ratios, performance indices, percentage completion all are indeed important. But they are not more important than accomplishing the purpose of the project by driving towards the right direction to meet the services needed by the customer.

The leadership transformation or anything for that matter in projects is a path that has to be traveled through. It is a journey, particularly when the project community is clinched on to management orientation for a long time, while other disciplines have evolved into leadership models. The 'personal management' has evolved as a 'human resources development' organization, which has gone through the transformation, but that did not happen overnight. In project management as well, we have miles to go to reach the leadership summit. It is great to see that there are a lot of thinkers and models moving in this direction. There are articles, books published, workshops conducted every year on this concept. It is a healthy trend to keep this movement going on. Organizations must invest in harnessing project leadership, to the same extent the project management was deployed a while ago. This is not only desirable but essential, particularly when the business is more relying on human potential to deliver value to the customers.

When did you last hear about a PMO, and when did you last overhear the term 'PLO,' if at all? - The "Project Leadership Organisation." PLO - Some of us might have not even known that terminology. Developing a leadership culture in organizations is complicated, particularly in a project environment. As the transformation journey of classical management to leadership, project management to project leadership also has its hardships to succeed in this direction. A leadership journey is not about turning the switch on, but it is a lifelong journey. There is a dire need for organizations to practice unconventional practices to create value from projects. There needs to be a shift in the skillsets, mindset, and toolset of how projects are merely managed to a level of leadership. This includes the following

Skillsets

From controlling chaos to developing mastery
Hard and fast rules/regulations to Agile and nimble guidelines
From 'chasing a wild goose' to 'in pursuit of the purpose.'
From project completion to delivery orientation
From passing on the buck to mutual accountability
From carrot and stick to passion propelled

Mindset

From control to latitude to operate
From blame culture to learning culture
From coordination to driving
From regulation to empowerment
From mistake-proof to a learning culture
From passing on the buck to trusted partners

Toolset

From controlling KPIs to unleashing potential
From time control to build for speed
From cost control to value creation
From a rigid scope to customer centricity
Reporting to Proacting

For the purpose of this book, I have conducted a survey among colleagues and peers on their thoughts on project leadership. These are all experienced project managers who drive projects day in day out in their assignments. Most of them have a fair understanding of the intricacies of projects. All of them viewed the project leadership differently, yet there is a common thread that is running in the thought process, which is a people-centric, purpose-driven, and voluntarily engaged workforce.

The Vector

Lack of direction, not lack of time, is the problem. We all have 24-hour days. — Zig Ziglar

---

The efforts are not recognized as much as the results are. Hence in life or business, the benefits realization remains an area to be focused upon. In this fast-paced world, where there is only a little time for doing everything, the time spent well in each of the aspects of the project matters a lot. This means the time spent is resulting in the expected benefits or results.

Hence completing the tasks that are in alignment with the results is a critical success factor. A task in the direction towards the purpose of a project is taking that business closer to the results or benefits. A task that is completed, which does not move the project an inch closer to the objectives is timewasters and will not be a factor of the project progress.

Once, a patient visited a dentist with a painful tooth, which was bothering him for a while, and wanted to solve that. After the diagnosis, the dentist informed that there is no way to save the teeth, it needs to be extracted in order to protect other teeth and for his oral hygiene. Cutting the story short, the dentist quoted a hundred dollars for this task.

The patient asked, "How much time it would take?".

The dentist said, "It would take one minute to extract the teeth." Annoyed the patient said the dentist,

"Are you serious, are you asking for 100 dollars for one minute. Do you know how much people are paid for the more complicated and time-consuming task than just extraction of damn teeth?"

The dentist replied,

"No worries son, I can take as much as time you like, but remember the more time I take, the more painful it is."

A dentist's effectiveness is in achieving his task in the shortest period of time. In projects as well, the quality of time spent in effectively completing the work is essential rather than the quantity of time consumed in achieving the same job.

Hence in business, the efforts are not to be measured, but the results are. This is similar to a vector, which is a measurement of both magnitude and direction. For instance, research and development of a new novel product, there could be many iterations that need to be done to accomplish an invention. While the iterations until the penultimate one result in learning, the last one takes the project towards the finish line. The iterations are still necessary as a part of the development, but the progress indeed determines the successful iteration. While the team is encouraged to do essential iterations needed, it can't be a wandering generality but focused on specific iterations which are in the direction of the results is necessary. Even for exploratory research, research centers nowadays use the design of the experiment to ensure that the efforts are focused on the meaningful progress of the project.

How to eat an elephant, a byte by byte, hence any larger objective or goal can be systematically divided into smaller pieces and sequentially handled in order to attain this through the vector. Every single task, which is connected to the purpose or objectives, is productive and leads to the headway of the project. Hence the vector is an essential factor when it comes to setting your priorities if one has several tasks that need to be done, then the most important task is the one in the right direction that needs to be taken up first. The vector guides the team on the journey towards the goals.

Part 4:

Toolkit

Part 6

The reality is that quite often what we need is small things that make a big difference. When David had to face off with Goliad, he did not have a sophisticated army or arsenal, instead, a simple sling with five stones, that was used to drive away from the birds from the harvest. Similarly, we have evidence that many times in business as well, small refinements one makes and practice on a day-to-day basis, give a significant lead in terms of advancing their career.

These tools in a way, are not the ones that require a significant cultural shift or require the organization to turn around overnight, or need a massive training program. These are simple refinements, which one can start practicing without making a big deal about it. These are the tools, which can be practiced once someone determines to do so. Moreover, all these can be done at a personal level, to begin with rather than depending on others. So, practicing this is the will of a project manager who wanted to advance their careers towards a leadership path that could benefit themselves as well as the organization as a whole. These tools are a combination of the old and new schools of thought, time-tested and revolutionary, logical and crazy enough. All these nine tools are linked with numbers, so it's hard to forget and comes in handy to practice.

Single point of accountability

> *"The ancient Romans had a tradition:*
> *whenever one of their engineers constructed an*
> *arch, as the capstone was hoisted into place,*
> *the engineer assumed accountability for his*
> *work in the most profound way possible: he*
> *stood under the arch."*

> — *Michael Armstrong*

'Single Point of Accountability' is the 'Power of One', the first tool in the toolkit.

Story 6: Ram's Story of being democratic

Ramakrishna Iyer, also known as RAM by his US colleagues, is a young and energetic program manager. Being at the beginning of his career, he is full of beans, he fills the project team with his energy. He is a go-to person who is at the top of all the information and status concerning his projects. Ram is an inclusive person, which means he cannot leave anyone in meetings, in action planning, in brainstorming sessions. He wanted to have everyone in the project team for most of the discussions.

Ram is also having one of the essential qualities of a program manager to record minutes of meetings and action plans to track it through.

115

Because of his inclusive nature, many times Ram adds multiple people to his action list. Every action will have three or four people assigned as responsible resources. Sometimes activities get closed without his follow-up. The few times he has to follow through with the people who are responsible to close the action point. As every task has 3 or 4 stakeholders as responsible people against his action list, he used to follow it up with one after another. Sometimes the first person has an answer, several times has to go until the end of the list to get actions closed. Like in a quiz, people had the option of passing the question to the next one. Having a higher amount of energy level and extroversion, Ram did not mind making several phone calls. There were few action items, where he has included a stakeholder and his supervisor and his manager, that is multiple people on the same team as responsible people. Yet at a certain point of time, Ram realized that eventually, this is not an efficient way of logging actions, as this leads to

a) increase the burden of follow-up with multiple people,

b) make him run around several people to close activity and

c) he is not able to hold somebody accountable if an action point has not been closed on time.

Indeed, Ram needs more responsible people in his organization and particularly in his projects who can own several deliverables. A project is about executing numerous tasks that are interlinked with each other to create the product services or results, which we call 'network.' In any project environment, it is common that there is some kind of template of action planning which is practiced, starting from a simple spreadsheet to complicated enterprise project scheduling systems.

Also, several action items would be emanating from various meetings and brainstorming sessions. Having a single person accountable for each of the action items is indeed essential to get things done successfully. Having multiple resources accountable for action or task will lead to diluting the responsibility. Hence it is essential to have a "one person" accountable for each action item to have full ownership and accountability – which makes the execution seamless. Not one department, not one function, it is the **Single Person Accountable** for completing every task. This single person accountable is abbreviated as SPA.

When a project manager drives the project through, there are tasks and action items that would get closed, also due to the progressive elaboration nature of the projects there are multiple tasks, and action items get generated as well. Many times there is a tendency to have multiple resources or a department assigned as responsible for delivering the same. Having multiple people accountable creates ambiguity in the system and dilutes accountability. When there is more than a single person assigned to a task, one might think that it is others' responsibility. Hence it is essential to assign a single person accountable for delivering each of these tasks. Multiple people's accountability means no one is accountable.

In a real-world scenario, there are indeed aspects that need to be performed by more than a single person. This can be achieved by splitting the activity into more granular pieces that can be assigned to two individuals. In case of inability to divide it further, it is essential to discuss with those multiple resources and to align with a single person as a SPA on behalf of the entire team. While multiple people can carry out an activity and can be responsible for the same, a single person needs to be held as an accountable person. That SPA bears the consequences of the success or failure of that particular aspect of the project.

I learned this from a CEO of a large multinational pharma organization I worked with, and let me provide the example which he has given to depict the power of single-point accountability. When you are traveling in flight, you might notice several people are working together to prepare for the journey. There are different teams like cockpit and cabin crews, airline operations center, maintenance and ground crew, flight deck crew, pushback crew, air traffic control working together starting from planning for the trip, fueling, food, and beverages, boarding the passengers and take off. Many people coming together and support to have a safe and comfortable travel experience. However, in this entire episode, who is the single point accountable for that flight? It is indeed the captain of the plane. The captain of the aircraft holds the complete accountability of ensuring that the aircraft is ready for the trip. The captain cannot have excuses on the midair that the flight was not fueled adequately by the team which is responsible for doing so. He or She can neither blame that the landing gear not working correctly. While there are multiple people responsible for doing several preparatory things, ultimately a single person holds the accountability for the flight. This is the power of sole point accountability. As a captain cannot blame others in the midair for the half-filled fuel, it will be equally dangerous for the project resources to dilute the accountability to several others. The captain becomes the sole responsible person for that particular journey, and he used the checklist and his leadership to ensure things are delivered before deciding for taking off. While all other team members are helping him to achieve that objective.

Similarly, in projects also there are multiple people and multiple teams that are working on a deliverable. However, it is essential for us to identify a single is accountable for that particular delivery. This improves accountability as well as coordination and decision-making. This also provides clarity between the team members. The project manager can ask a question to the SPA if things are not happening. The single-person accountability is not just limited to the people who execute the project. There are there levels of accountability we can deal with within a project environment.

A. **Project accountability**: at the global level, the one who holds the accountability of the entire project. B. **Asset owners**: at the domain level, the owner of each and every segment of the project C. **Task accountability**: At the task level, the one who is responsible for executing the task.

Project Accountability: Project accountability is about the one who is accountable for the success or failure of the project. We often are tempted to have a steering committee, project boards, which comprises multiple leaders, this is pertinent specifically in a matrix organization. However, it is sufficient to have a single person from those leadership teams assigned as a SPA for the success of the project as a representative of the leadership team. This will create a tremendous level of clarity when it comes to decision-making.

The project accountability can be with the project sponsor. Often this is the single person who sets the vision of the entire project. While a sponsor cannot get involved in driving the project on day to day basis, the same can be delegated to an individual leader who can be involved in the day-to-day affairs of the project and be available to the team for solving problems when needed.

The purpose of the existence of the product can be consistently ensured by this single person. Hence the team can come to this person to go, no-go decision whenever there is a conflict with respect to the product viability. This person holds the strategic accountability of the project and becomes a critical decision-maker in ambiguous situations.

Asset owners: These are the people who are responsible for executing various work packages of the project. Quite often the asset owners are department heads, unit heads, or the ones who is having domain expertise. They are the vital link between vision and execution. They translate a project vision into reality. These people bring-in clarity on the tactical execution aspect of the project. They commit their resources and the funds needed to execute several sections of the project. They play a vital role in terms of deciding the velocity of overall execution. They own the resources that are deployed for the project in various phases.

Projects required functional and technical expertise throughout the life cycle of the project. The execution rigor is determined by asset owners at each stage. Hence it is important to hold accountable for the respective phase of the project or each of the assets. The asset owners need to work closely with their fellow asset owners of other phases of the projects.

It is a common practice to have several asset owners play a lead role in various phases of a project. For a new product development project, the chief of R&D has a predominant role at the beginning of the project, and the head of operations has an important part in the end game. So, it is vital to define this upfront, and have them committed to the overall plan of the project and hold them accountable as well.

Task Level Accountability: These are the resources, who find their names in each of the WBS of a Gantt chart or assigned against each of the action points in a minute of meeting or risk log. They belong to the core execution team of the project and very important in progress. Hence it is vital to have a single person assigned to each of the action points and to disambiguate the accountability.

Try out this: Next time in an action planning meeting, instead of writing a department name as an action owner, start writing a single name as a SPA and see the difference. Once a particular name is on the cards, people tend to take ownership and deliver or at least improve the response. Though it might differ from organization to organization based on the project management maturity model and culture, commonly using 'individual names' is an effective way to get accountability from a team, group or department.

Useful Tools: RACI Chart

RACI chart is a time-tested tool that comes in handy in defining the responsibility and communication matrix.

RACI charts are used to clearly identify who has to do what is related to the detailed steps in a project.

The RACI chart summarizes the key tasks in the form of action items. Each task may need the involvement of several people. The RACI chart clarifies what type of engagement is necessary for all of those involved. The definitions below explain what the four definitions mean in terms of people's participation.

Each task may have several people who are responsible (R) need to be consulted (C) or informed (I) however can only have one person per task who can be accountable(A). A person can be Responsible and Accountable for the same task

Example:

CONCEPTS, DESIGN AND DOCUMENTS COMMUNICATION CHART

Company Name
Project Name:
Location:

Rev:
Date:
By:

(See last page for Notes)	PMO			Build			Technical			Quality				Others			
R = Responsible A = Approval /Accountable C = Consulted/Involved I = Informed	Tom (Project Sponsor)	John (PMO)	Robert (Ops PMO)	Bob (Operations)	Kenny (Global engineering)	Watson (Build Team)	Will (Tech Transfer)	Smit (Research and Development)	Manny (Start-up)	Gilbert (Quality Assurance)	Rick (Analytical)	Mohmad (Tech Operations)	Kate (EHS)	Williams (Project Procurement)	Phillip (Human Resources)	Raj (Information Technology)
Safety																
EHS System Design and Review docum	A	I	I	R	R	C				C			R	I		
On Site/Offsite Emergency Prepardnes	A	I	I	R	R	C				C			R	I	I	
Permits & Other Communications with Government Agencies	A	C	C	R	R	C				R					I	
Site Safety Construction Metrices	I	C	C	R	R/A	C				C			R	I		
Pre-commissioning Safety Metrices	I	C	C	R/A	R	C				C			R	I		

Figure 10: RACI Chart

Responsibility Definitions

R Responsible The doers. The person or persons directly involved in performing the activity per defined procedure and impacting the results. These people are responsible for performing the task and accountable for their actions

A Accountable The buck stops here. The person with the ultimate authority. 'Accountable' ensures that the policies and procedures are adhered to, the process is measured, exceptions are monitored, etc. Is the lowest level person who has the authority to change the process.

C Consult The reference points, the person or persons who must be consulted or whose opinion must be obtained before a decision is made.

I Inform The need to know. The person or persons who should be actively informed of decisions or outcomes. Passive information

Who is the SPA in the RACI matrix? It is the A the one who holds the accountability and becomes a SPA for that particular task.

Now having established a single point of accountability, the next tool is about having focused meetings, which increase the ability of a project manager to drive a project.

Two Pizza Rule.

Ram, whom we have seen in the last chapter, is also having a habit of calling everyone for meeting with a good intention to make people aware of what's going on in the projects. His underlying intent is not to leave anyone out of the loop, when there are certain decisions are made. This leads to good collaboration between the team. However, the burden of organizing meetings, conducting that effectively, and closing out becoming increasingly cumbersome day by day. Because of the number of participants, several times the sessions run over. There are few times wherein the meeting is not focused, but there are several tangential points put forward for resolution. Each individual who is at the meeting wanted to mark their presence. Hence they tend to come up with a couple of points, which could get the place in the minutes of the meeting. The meetings are becoming a sort of chaotic event that requires a lot of energy to conduct.

Moreover, as days go by, several leaders started complaining that they have too many project meetings to attend. Even some of the resources who execute the project, feel that in a day have more time spent on meetings rather than doing the work that they are assigned. Ram's 360-degree feedback as part of the annual appraisal had a lot of suggestions on reducing the number of meetings, quorum, and durations of sessions and allow people to focus on projects. Indirectly it means for him that he needs to minimize the overdose of 'project management' on to the team. It is a fact that he got a little disappointed in this feedback, all that is done is with good intention to make everyone participate, be in the loop, and have their say.

Meetings are one of the vital collaboration mechanisms in which project leaders communicate the progress, facilitate decisions, and drive the projects. Particularly when it comes to innovation or technology-dominant projects, people are the key drivers of the project and hence needed to be included.

Amazon's Jeff Bezos is popularly known for the application of two Pizza rule for conducting productive meetings. The two-pizza rule is a guiding principle for defining the maximum number of participants in a meeting. According to the rule, a meeting should not have more attendees than all of them could not be fed with two pizzas. Generally, this limits the number of participants at a meeting to less than eight.

Project meetings are not a democratic process wherein one needs to get buy-in from all. However, it is essential to have decisions, and escalations communicated up and down to the appropriate level. Very often, project managers end up having this dilemma, and to include all participants in their meeting, relevant or irrelevant, in effect, the meeting becomes a consensus gathering process. For effective decision-making, it is always appropriate to have focused subgroup meetings to gain consensus and to float the recommendations up to the next level to achieve further alignment. Many times there is a temptation to have interdisciplinary group meetings by including everyone involved in the process from various functions. The basis of this is to keep everyone engaged, and also this acts as a team-building exercise. Well, this is appropriate when carried out infrequently like once a year or for an annual planning meeting or kind of town hall meeting. But while executing a project, for project governance, large meetings are not needed.

For your project, work out a precise governance mechanism of information flow. This might include an arrangement in which the issues and decision requests are raised, and the decisions, solutions, approvals, and grants are cascaded down. The intent is not to make this process bureaucratic, but to work out an enabling process to utilize the strength of the leadership team and the execution teams. Also, a point that must be noted is that the visibility will be better as we got higher and higher, leaders will be able to see a larger perspective. The main focus of this process needs to be not having any lag but to resolve issues quickly and make the decision-making process nimble.

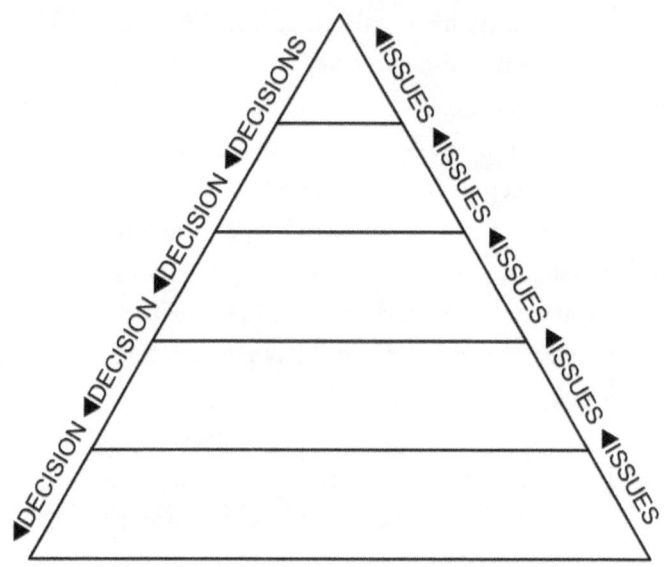

Figure 12: Issues and Decisions Flow in Meetings

Once the 'two pizza' kind of mechanism is instituted, it does not anymore require overwhelming discussions. Instead, the decision-making process becomes lean, and the team operates with a higher velocity. The following are some of the guiding principles that can be considered while designing the meeting's cadence.

- Meetings are not for the status update (can be done over a report)
- Smaller the better
- Must have agenda or frequency
- Respect everyone's time
- Start on time, conclude on time
- Follow-through
- Never over-discuss or repeat
- Don't problem solve if the intent is not the same

- Close before time if it is done
- Don't push for decisions when decision-makers are unavailable
- Use the parking lots effectively
- Make people accountable for actions
- Have pre-reads available much before the meetings as well.

Often when the meetings run over the scheduled timeline, it becomes counterproductive. This results in not utilizing everyone's time judicially. Having 50 members in extravagant discussion mean that 50-man-hours is wasted even if it is one single hour meeting. Time spent on each of these resources comes at a cost as well as the progress the team needs to make on the respective tasks. This time is not available for the team members to work on the projects. Hence project leaders need to identify the touchpoints of the people who will be involved in daily, weekly, monthly, quarterly, and annual meetings and then have those people highly engaged in active discussion. Remember not to have more than 8 people available at any point in time for effective meetings.

The level at which the things to be discussed is lesser at the bottom of the pyramid when you compare it with the top. Top-level often requires a thirty thousand feet level view so that they will be able to take an effective decision. Also, they wanted to make sure that everyone in the pyramid is involved and be a part of the system.

Try out this:

Next time when you are tempted to have a larger meeting, try to have a subgroup to do pre-works as a preparation for the meeting. Go to the meeting with validated actions or decisions and communications. Organize for the next level of the meeting, and so on to a level in which the decision needs to be endorsed.

Have a well-defined project communication plan along with project scope documents. Ensure that the groups are defined at various levels like a steering committee, working-level group, leadership, and task workstream groups. This will be a useful tool to get the best out of every team as the focus and granularity would be different at each phase.

Now having fixed the SPA and streamlined the meetings, the next tool is about playing around the triple constraints and opportunities, which target to improve the efficiency of the project or unleash the true potential of people.

Tool

3

Leverage Triple Opportunities

Triple constraint is one of the lucid ways which depicted the three most important factors that determined the success of the project, that is executed in the industrial age. This simply states that one can't be altered without affecting others. This is obvious that a leader has a look at all parameters of the triple constraint to make a project successful per the pre-determined objectives. It is essential for the project manager to have this well-defined in the project charter and to have a consistent calibration of this while progressing the projects. Many times when the project is progressively elaborated, there could be additional aspects that get uncovered. This is more prevalent in today's situation as more and more projects are an intellectual process rather than brick-and-mortar type.

Triple constraints are still relevant for some of your brick and mortar projects, where efficiency matters. Control is appropriate for machines, and release is appropriate for human potential. In cognitive projects, there is a tremendous opportunity for turning around the triple constraints to triple opportunities. The summary is, we engage triple opportunities which include a) creating value out of every step, b) increase the velocity of the project rather than controlling the time, and c) always align with the purpose of the project rather than having arbitrary scope definition.

Here are the differences between triple constraints and triple opportunities.

Triple constraints	Triple Opportunities
Applicable for brick and mortar projects	Applicable for the knowledge era
Physical work	Cognitive work
Efforts create results	The effort is not directly proportional to results
Control	Release
Efficiency	Potential
More dependence on machine	More dependence on cognition
Hard and fast rules	Flexible: in fact, no rules, but freedom to operate
Discipline	Agile and nimble
Conditional employment	Voluntary engagement
Predictable	Vulnerable, Uncertain, Complex, and Ambiguous

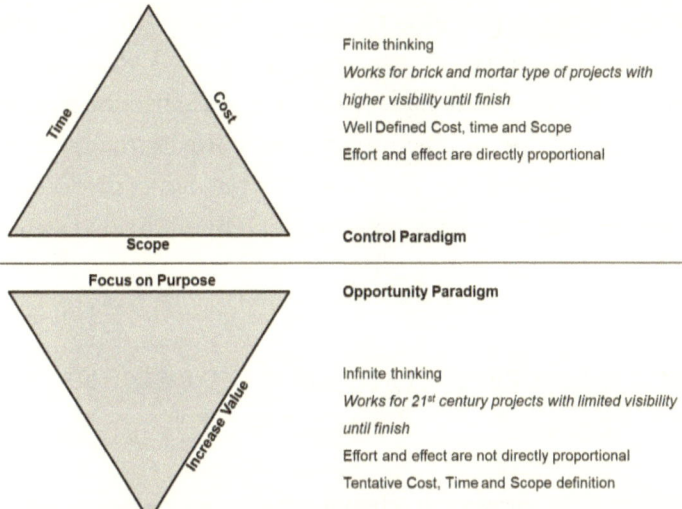

Figure 13: Transforming Triple Constraints from Control Paradigm to Opportunity Paradigms

Triple Opportunity Worksheet

Project is a process that converts ideas into products, services, and results through a systematic, step-by-step creative process. The core of the project is the purpose of the project. That is the very reason for the existence of a project. Once the purpose is established, the same can be delivered to bring out the best possible product at the maximum velocity and enhanced value.

Use the following tool to undertake the journey from the constraint paradigm to the opportunity paradigm. Fill out the following questionnaire for your projects. For every imperative, there is a scale provided. 10 indicates the best, and 1 indicates the starting point. Mark the spot in pencil where you or your organization is right now as 'P' indicating 'Present' and 'D' indicating 'Desirable' state in a particular period. Discuss this with your manager and

133

teams. Work out actions for improvement. These actions will become initiatives that propel you and your team's journey towards leadership. Don't try to change the culture overnight, it does not happen that way. Revisit the list after a certain period to calibrate if you have made any improvement in your approach which might have resulted in the organizational maturity

IMPERATIVES TO TRANSFORM DEADLINE TO VELOCITY:

Some of the systematic changes in the project ecosystem would lead to an enabling environment to increase the velocity of a cognitive project. Consider some velocity maximizers from the examples provided below:

S. No	Velocity Imperatives	1	2	3	4	5	6	7	8	9	10
1.	Clear decisions are made for uninterrupted progress										
2.	A highly capable and inspired workforce completes the tasks faster										
3.	Vividly defined Accountability and responsibility										
4.	Direct involvement of the execution team in planning										
5.	Able to respond to internal and external development that might hamper the project consistently										
6.	Practicing mono-tasking to improve the delivery										
7.	Turnaround times (TAT) defined for every interface and increasing service levels										
8.	Seamless integration between workstreams that reinforces interdependency										
9.	The project team is empowered to make decisions										
10.	Bench strength or additional resources available in case of need										
11.	Working out watertight schedules for activities that are conspicuous										
12.	Upfront definitions of the way forward are given in the case of 'if-else' scenarios to avoid ambiguity										

134

		1	2	3	4	5	6	7	8	9	10	11	12
13.	Clear communication and collaboration												
14.	Avoidance of communication crusade that saps time and energy of resources												
15.	Expert groups or subject matter experts (SMEs) available for specific jobs for focused, faster delivery												
16.	Full Kitting Checklists: Not idling for the input material												
17.	Availability of bench strength or additional resources depending on the need of the project												
18.													
19.													
20.													

Define the initiatives or actions that you will initiate in order to improve the Velocity of projects

_____

_____

_____

_____

_____

_____

_____

_____

_____

_____

_____

_____

IMPERATIVES TO TRANSFORM FROM 'CONTROLLING COST' TO 'MAXIMIZING THE VALUE.'

The following are some examples of the value-maximizing imperatives in a project environment:

S. No	Value Imperatives	1	2	3	4	5	6	7	8	9	10

1.	Better utilization of capacities in the interest of obtaining optimum returns from available project resources										
2.	Reduction in the number of iterations/ obsolescence, and passing on of the cost advantage to the customer or sponsor										
3.	Use of latest technologies in the project; use of the latest materials, methods, and knowledge										
4.	Improving the quality of delivery at every step, which enhances the quality of the project as a whole										
5.	Focus on improving the product's core purpose rather than working on ancillary benefits										
6.	Identification and pruning of unviable projects at early stages, failing early and, thus, failing cheap										
7.	Increased productivity from resources committed to project										
8.	Reducing total cost of ownership										
9.	Use of economies of scale to reduce cost										
10.	Better utilization of capacities in the interest of obtaining optimum returns from available project resources										
11.	Use of SMEs to maximize the value of individual steps										
12.											
13.											
14.											
15.											
16.											
17.											
18.											
19.											
20.											

Define the initiatives or actions that you will initiate in order to improve the Value of each and every step of the project

_____

_____

_____

_____

_____

_____

_____

Imperatives to transforming arbitrary scope definition to Purpose: Following are some imperatives that enable focus on purpose rather than a rigid scope framework:

S. No	Purpose Imperatives	1	2	3	4	5	6	7	8	9	10
1.	A clear, unambiguous definition of the purpose of the project										
2.	Focus on the purpose of the project at every stage of the project—all other attributes are either input to the project or additional outcomes; consistent recalibration of the project course to align it with the purpose										
3.	Harnessing unfolding opportunities due to technological development										
4.	Fostering purpose-centric project ecosystems										
5.	Focusing on developing high-quality products, services, or results										
6.	Focusing on the true north and not on parameters										
7.	Engagement of center of excellence										
8.	Uncomplicated scope change practices that make changes possible, if needed										
9.	Make bench strength and contingent investment accessible to project teams, if necessary										
10.	Focused mini-project teams with clear accountability and faster decisions										
11.	Incentives and KPIs being aligned with the purpose of the project										
12.	Leveraging eureka moments to benefit from it for projects										
13.	Fostering the creative process for the sake of gaining maximum benefit from it										
14.	A vision map is created for every project										
15.	Handling unplanned tasks due to the progressive elaboration										
16.	Responding to internal and external development that might hamper the project										
17.											
18.											
19.											
20.											

Define the initiatives or actions that you will initiate in order to focus on the Purpose of projects

_____

_____

_____

_____

_____

_____

_____

_____

_____

_____

_____

Now having fixed the SPA, effective meetings, and able to create triple opportunities amidst the constrained world, the next tool is about making a precise presentation, the status report of a project on one page!

Tool

4

The Four-up's

I had a colleague who is an expert in technology transfer. Once, we had a review meeting with the executive director, and he wanted to review all the delayed projects. One of the projects is a pharmaceutical generic product development of diabetes medicine. This product was developed successfully at the R&D center but has quite a few scale-up issues at the pilot plant. My friend, chief of technology transfer workstream, was dealing with this. He has prepared a slide deck with 182 pages, which has all nuances about the product, to the extent of explaining how the bonds break and infuse with another structure to make the desired molecule structure. The executive director himself is a scientist, and he worked his way through on the corporate ladder with his technical excellence. Intrigued by this presentation, the discussion went on. But it was not too late when he collected himself and had to stop the presentation saying that, this is too much detailed and all that he needs is an executive summary, with an action plan for a recovery of this failing project.

Many times the project managers tend to over detail or underplay the status update of the projects. Either way, it is not going to be useful for the review. All that is needed for a project review from the executive sponsor something which connects the past, future, concerns, and decision requests.

One of my project management mentors enlightened me that "if your presentation is not understandable to your daughter who is in eighth grade, then this will not be understood by your sponsors". Often, we try to complicate the presentation with an overload of information. An eye for details is indeed critical while driving the project, yet this may not be necessary at all levels and mainly when one wanted to assess the status of the project from 30,000 feet level. I was in search of a one-page summary that explains the status of the project as a debrief, yet has all essential components included in it. The answer to my quest is the 'four up' reporting of the project.

While there are many dashboards, loads of complicated charts that can be used to illustrate the status of a project, the four up is interestingly a simple tool. When it comes to project reporting, it is always better to be a single-page report rather than voluminous information. Particularly in today's world, where everything needs to be precise and accurate, project leaders need to communicate the status of the project on one page.

For a project status review, there are four clusters of information which is critical a) the current status of the project, b) risks and issues c) what is that we are going to do in the next few months or days - depending on the length of the project, and d) any key decision which is needed. All these can be presented on a single page in the form called four ups, one quadrant for each of them, in a simple slide which can be created in PowerPoint or Word document or whiteboard or whatever software tool you are using for reporting your progress.

Quadrant 1: project status update and progress since the last update (if this is a periodic review)

Quadrant 2: Issues/Risks and Decision requests

Quadrant 3: Activities for the next period

Quadrant 4: Milestone list and status update

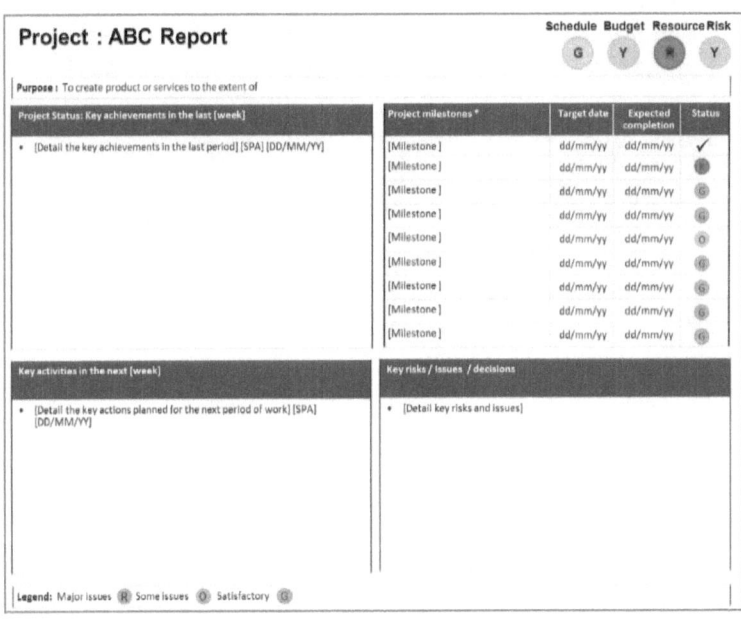

Figure 14: The Four ups

While there are tons of information available in every project, we don't have time to synthesize that in every meeting. The four up, on the other hand, is an executive-level summary that depicts the big picture of a project. This enables the focus of the team towards the most important issues and action-oriented.

TIPS: If your organization has a habit of lengthy presentations, use these 4 ups as a 'landing' slide. You may find that this will be able to cover most of the information, and the review effectiveness goes up.

The first four tools are on accountability, productive meetings, leverage opportunity paradigm, and making crystal clear project update, the next tool is about the ability to deep dive into issues to find the root cause.

Tool

5

Why-Five's

Projects have an overwhelming share of problem-solving to be done. One of the critical competencies is to get to the core of every issue to resolve them entirely rather than a surface-level symptomatic fix. The Why-Five's help project leaders to get to the bottom of the problems that hamper the project, be it problems, scope creep, or decisions. Like Wi-Fi connects to the internet, the Why-Five's, a fancy title for the classic 'five whys' tool helps to deep dive to the core of everything in projects for a leader.

Five whys, a classical tool, but not popular for managing projects. One of my mentors insisted on the use of this in projects. After an initial reluctance, I started using it for finding out the root causes of project impediments. My experience is that it takes one to get to the core of the issues instantaneously and helps effectively resolve them. The role of project leaders in today's project is more of problem-solving than coordinating and following up. Mainly when the multiple project teams are working across geographies in a project.

Let's look at the genesis of five whys as a technique. Five whys have been developed initially as an interrogative

143

technique used to establish a cause and effect relationship in identifying a problem. This technique was formally developed and used in Toyota Motor Corporation during the evaluation of the Toyota Manufacturing System, which revolutionized the manufacturing systems. When it was initially designed, the method has not been attached to any hard and fast rule but only intended to deep dive until the identification of the root cause of the problem to resolve.

Let us look at how it is relevant to today's projects. Sometimes, today's projects tend to start with very loosely defined objectives which eventually get into the project charter. Based on this, when a project team starts executing a project, they end up with several change requests before concluding. These change requests are originated from the customer as well as project teams. These are typically tagged as 'scope creeps.' This, in turn, makes the project exceed the budget or extend the timeline from the original estimate. This is a result of defining the attributes of a project rather than defining the purpose as scope. There is an urban legend that demonstrates the power of understanding the purpose of the project. The story goes like this. The United States developed a cryogenic propelled artificial intelligent pen, which can work in space. When they approach the Soviet Union to market this product, they got a reply from the Soviet Union that they don't use pens in the space; instead, they use pencils.

It is indeed, essential for every project team to understand the core purpose needed to be achieved through the project. Many times the purpose of a project itself is answering a question or solving a problem. Hence from the project charter onwards, the five whys are very relevant.

While applying the five whys in project defining the scope, one of the byproducts of this approach is that this makes the scope definition more customer-centric rather than defining something which is business inferred. This, in turn, would minimize the scope changes, by reducing the gap between what customers wanted and how a project is conceived. This will drive the entire project words focusing on the purpose of the project, remember the example of 'quarter-inch hole' by Harvard professor Theodore Levitt.

Five whys establish tremendous learning for other projects which are of the same nature, and the lessons learned in one project can be applied to another. This adds value in pre-empting certain typical setbacks in the project also a steep learning curve of the project team to solve them.

The first five tools are linked with one, two, three, four, and five. Now that the trend is known, can we make a guess the choice for the sixth? Is that the six phases of a project, namely, 1. Enthusiasm, 2. Disillusionment, 3. Panic, 4. Search for the guilty, 5. Punishment of the innocent and 6. Praise and honors for the non-participants! Google got me this strange result for one of my searches - someone might have got seriously stifled by triple constraints.

The sixth one is an effort towards the holistic improvement of project leadership maturity.

Project's Six Sigma

Six Sigma (6σ) is a set of management techniques intended to improve business processes by significantly reducing the probability that an error or defect will occur. It was introduced at Motorola by their engineer Bill Smith in 1980. Jack Welch made it a nucleus to the business strategy in General Electric. From that time, several businesses embraced the six sigma and indeed created the desired results. A six sigma framework is the one which ensures statistically 99.99966% of the products are statistically expected to be free of defects.

But so far we clung to popular belief that a project is a temporary endeavor, where is the possibility of creating results which can target for that and how to implement a continuous improvement like six sigma in a temporary endeavor. Looks like an oxymoron, isn't it?

Let us take a deep dive into the six sigma fundamentals

A six sigma process assures

- Continuous endeavor to reducing process variation and attain stable and predictable process which are of essential to business success.
- Processes that have features that can be defined, measured, analyzed, improved, and controlled.
- Achieving sustained quality improvement that requires involvement and commitment from the entire organization, be it executive level management or at the shop floor.

Like manufacturing discipline achieved maturity to eliminate defects, projects too can travel the path of maturity continuum. Not all businesses are opting for a formal project governance model in the first instance. Yet, it is a necessity to create a formal structure of project governance in the organization, and there are multiple ways in which the structure gets shape based on evolution or even revolution. All that depends on how the projects are contributing to the growth of the core business. The project management as well is going through a shift, and it is time for us to have a real look at the practices which has been followed. Are the project management practices being compatible with the industrial era or it has been advanced to a knowledge workforce? Is this continuing to be a transactional system or getting evolved into a transformational workstream?

Story 7: Jack's PMO deployment

When John Brown, known to all as Big Jack, was hired by Widget Semiconductors he was given the responsibility and the opportunity to introduce formalized project management into an organization that, as you may have guessed, develops and manufactures semiconductors.

Big Jack was excited to be tackling this role, knowing that he was being given the rare opportunity to create a new system from scratch, and he couldn't wait to get started. The second reason for his excitement, as well as his trepidation, was that the in-house semiconductor program was the main engine of growth for Widget. It was the responsibility of the R&D team to develop new and innovative products that would then be transferred to the plants for commercial manufacture and ultimately to be supplied to customers.

The semiconductor industry is notorious for its rapid rate of technological obsolescence and its fierce competition. The survival of the company depended on a steady stream of new products coming to market on time. Being on time to market, ahead of competitor products was the key to commercial success. To enhance its ability to take the lead and to stay at the head of the pack, Widget recognized the importance of effective project management and hired Jack with a mandate to institute best practices of project management to reduce the time-to-market of its new product introductions.

The company already had several part-time project managers who primarily played the role of coordinators, but understood that there was a lot more to project management than logistics, and was willing to take whatever steps necessary to establish a top-notch project management organization. Big Jack had rich and varied experience in implementing formal project management processes in numerous organizations. However, the ace up his sleeve at Widget was that he had strong of the company leadership. Big Jack knew that for any project management system to be sustainable, buy-in from the sponsor as well as stakeholders was critical. His approach towards the successful deployment of PMOs was to establish rapport, institute systems, build credibility, produce results, and then move on to the next phase of implementation. He had a phase-wise deployment strategy, starting with a proper governance system and a fundamentally sound project schedule, risk register, and communication matrix.

On that day, Big Jack had a meeting lined up with Dr. Chris Parker, who was the head of the research and development wing. His objective for the meeting was to form a winning coalition with the R&D chief, and they had a fascinating discussion.

"So, Jack, I believe that I got all that you are saying. You want to institute a governance system, or in other words, a management system. You proposed to create formal schedules, risk registers, and phased reviews for the projects. All that is fine from a management perspective, but please help me understand how any of this will benefit my team and me to accelerate new product development. To be perfectly frank, what this looks like is just one more bureaucratic process imposed on the already onerous and painful project review systems. How would even more red tape drive the speed of development?" asked Chris.

"Chris, I fully understand your concerns!" answered Big Jack. "While at first blush the project management system I'm proposing looks purely administrative, as we progress and deploy the process, I am confident that you will soon recognize the impact of the discipline in execution on the rigor of your scientific development at every stage of the project. This will ultimately result in a clear direction to the team, which will help accelerate the development. These results have been proven time and again and are well documented. Furthermore, companies have really increased their performance by implementing best practices of project management."

Big Jack flipped through a few more slides from his presentation, which were taken from the reputed project institute's annual survey on the success rate of projects in companies implementing formal project management practices. The data showed unambiguously that companies have turned around their project performance by implementing formal project management practices.

"But visibility and governance are not our key problems. We already have two project managers tracking project progress. Our problem is the deep-rooted technical challenges, and as long as these challenges are not resolved, no amount of governance we put over the system will not help in accelerating development."

"Chris, I agree with you. No system is ever going to solve your technical problems. What it will help you to do is to understand as early as possible that you are likely to face a time crunch, and allow you to manage your budget and resources in such a way as to avoid that problem. In this way, you will have a system that does support you in the decisions you need to make. The project management system will not reduce complexity, but it helps to increase the capability to handle complexity."

The direction of the discussion was positive and healthy, and it was Big Jack's knowledge, confidence, and charisma, which enabled him to get the buy-in he needed to start achieving results. Jack went on collaborating with Dr. Parker, giving him significant help in deploying PMO. We wish him all the best.

The project governance practices as well following a maturity continuum, we can see this in four phases, namely a) Ad Hoc, b) Basic System, c) Project Management, and d) Project Leadership. In Projects, we can find all these four phases exist in organizations, depending on the value projects add to the business.

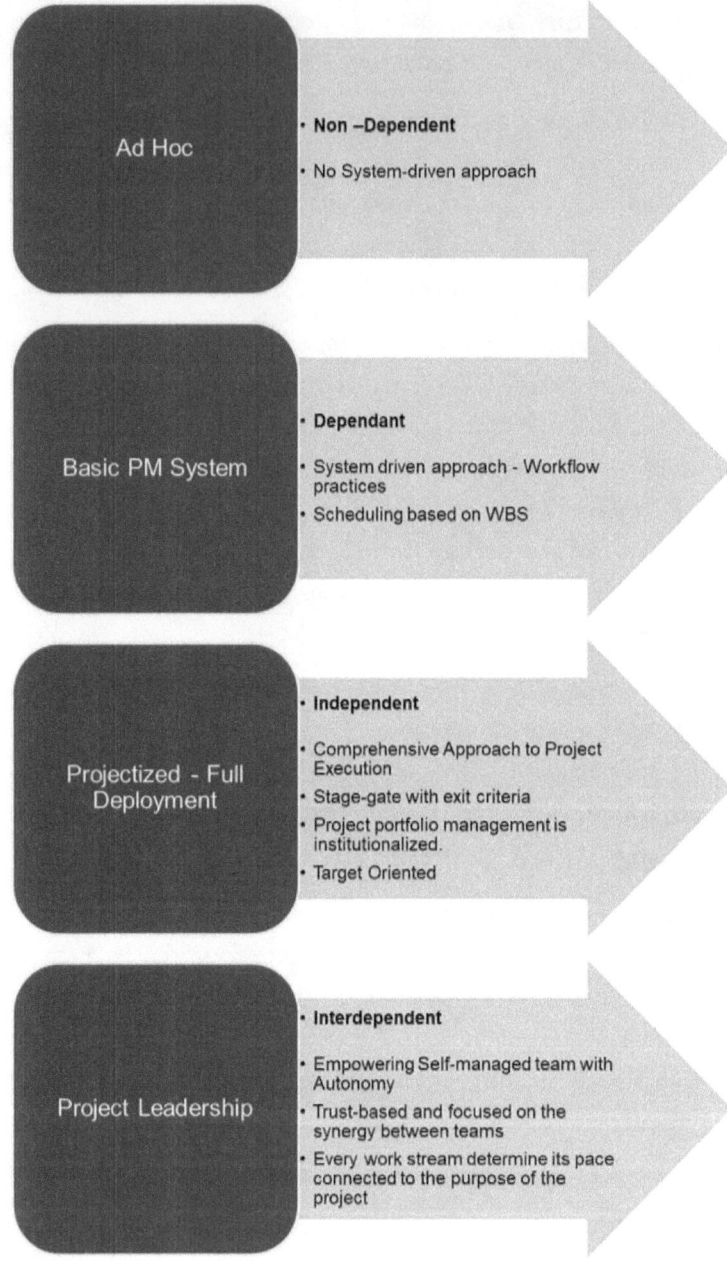

Figure 15: The Project Governance Maturity Model

STAGE 0: AD-HOC

This is as good as not recognizing the need for formal governance of projects as a discipline. This provides no or little system support for carrying our projects. No full-time project management structure exists in such a phase. This is because everything happens entirely right all the time or the portion of projects in the organization's portfolio is small, which needs very little to support a full-time PMO structure. While I try to sugarcoat this situation, everything happening right the first time is an ideal scenario, and a reduced portion of projects in the portfolio signifies that the business is in saturation mode and not growing. In reality, this happens because of less recognition of PMO as a discipline.

In such a scenario, projects are declared, and cross-functional team members are carved out from existing functions that already have a 'day job' to do. The assumption is everyone contributes their part to deliver the project. Still, projects can be delivered but not to the best of their potential. This leaves room for chaos and conflict between work streams and resources that need to contribute to the projects, which has their priority. You will find some part-time project coordinators crowned as project managers in such an environment. You will find a top leader pushing the project through power and authority. Back of the envelope planning, arbitrary target setting, and individual-based prioritization of tasks are the common traits

- No consistent formal process

- Informal approaches – each project is handled differently.
- Highly dominated by individuals
- No System-driven approach
- Working in silos
- Minimum established workflows
- Project outcomes unpredictable
- Unscientific schedules
- Parkinson's and Student Syndrome -Firefighting
- Little System Support
- What leader declare is the critical task

Focus: Somehow completing the project. Arbitrary targets and adrenaline-based push to progress the projects. The ability to 'firefight' and controlling chaos is valued most.

Pros: Uncomplicated or nil system, might work for small projects

Cons: Individual dominance, chaotic, no clear roles and responsibility, seldom challenging to carry out a cognitive project or even a large brick and mortar project

STAGE 1: BASIC PROJECT MANAGEMENT SYSTEMS:

This is a level when some basic discipline of planning and measurement of time and cost begins. Start of the use of scheduling techniques and software for planning that helps to determine a critical path to focus. Not all processes are documented. Projects are majorly tracked against time, and some of the cases cost as well. You will find full-time project managers, planners/schedulers in place.

- A basic systematic approach to project execution
- Organized support from project management
- Repeatable processes are applied
- Use of standard tools and techniques for a few project management processes
- Project Management methodology
- System driven approach - Workflow practices
- Scheduling based on WBS
- Basic project management training
- Standard Operating Procedures
- Short interval control

Focus: A Systematic way of completing the project. The project plan is valued most.

Pros: Functions driven, project scheduling helps them to track the progress.

Cons: Minimum formal, consistent system, lack of this does not guarantee the outcomes.

STAGE 2: PROJECT MANAGEMENT FULLY DEPLOYED: ADVANCED CONTROLS

This is the next level with the implementation of consistent formal processes that enable good project governance. Formal Scope change system, granular, risk-adjusted project schedules, earned value analysis is deployed to measure and track KPIs to a precision. Most of the processes are documented. You will find a full PMO organization here, which is controlling every piece of the project.

- A comprehensive approach to project execution
- History of previous project learnings are maintained and utilized
- Team and project managers trained in project management
- Consistent use of tools and techniques for project management processes
- Stage-gate with exit criteria
- Document everything starting from project initiation to closure, acceptance, feasibility check, scope change, technology, handover
- Project portfolio management is institutionalized.
- The organization can efficiently plan, manage, integrate and control multiple projects
- Project management environment improvement is actively encouraged project-centered organization structure
- Completely System driven approach
- Active senior management support for the integration of business planning and project execution
- Project-driven Organization

Focus: Project-centric: achieving targets, KPIs, meeting every intermediate milestone, sophisticated IT systems, and spreadsheet, delivering the Project as per the pre-determined scope is valued most.

Pros: Formal, consistent system targeting for accuracy to measure KPIs of projects, role clarity, communication matrix. Relevant for massive construction projects to innovation and cognitive projects.

Cons: Overwhelming controls stifles innovation and do not offer flexibility. The flipside of the system-driven approach is the development of bureaucracy and inertia within workstreams

STAGE 3: PROJECT LEADERSHIP

This is the level that we try to reinstate through this book. This is about having purpose-centric, customer-focused project teams that are motivated to perform the tasks to create value out of their role. Self-managed teams drive the project, and the interfaces between work streams are strengthened and seamless. Projects are driven by interdependent trams and local optima to drive global optima,

- Empowering Self-managed team with autonomy
- Identify bottlenecks and improve
- Interdependency to drive a multitude of the project through mini-projects, seamless integration of workstreams
- Trust-based and focused on the synergy between teams
- Delivery management teams
- No micromanagement, workstreams have their latitude to operate in line with the purpose of the project
- Every workstream determines its pace connected to the purpose of the project

Focus: Purpose centric, creating value, the customer is valued most

Pros: Offers autonomy and velocity, suitable for cognitive projects and human-dependent works, empowerment of the people, agile and nimble practices, no authority, but trust-based culture.

Cons: Does not support micromanagement, which eventually does not support overwhelming metrics and measurements. Not suitable for the project that depends on machines such as brick and mortar projects.

There is a reason why in projects the professionals are clichéd on to the management model for a long time. As the projects are temporary, it needs to yield the benefits realization in a shorter time. There was not adequate time for looking after the inherent leadership aspects, these are taken for granted. But in today's situation, the projects are perpetual, and project teams are part of the organization for a long gestation. Hence it is vital to focus on this six-sigma journey in projects to attain the leadership level.

Features that positioned Six-Sigma a notch above comparing to other quality-improvement initiatives are:

- Focussed on achieving quantifiable financial returns
- Involvement of senior leadership.
- Data-based decision than assumptions and guesswork.

Given that this can be adapted to the projects, this can indeed start turning the way in which projects are governed and improve the reliability of the projects, customer satisfaction, and benefits realization.

Tool

7

Seven Cardinal Rules of a Leader

Stephan Covey has written a winning formula known as seven habits of highly effective people, which helped millions to enhance their work and life; I was certainly one of them who benefited from such a concept. What could be the seven habits of highly effective leaders in projects? I was searching for the gurus in this space to get a set of characteristics that are needed to be inculcated by anyone who wants to become an effective project leader.

I stumbled upon **Dr. A.P.J. Abdul Kalam, Former President of India**, addressing the gathering at Project Management National Conference 2011. These seven cardinal rules are derived not only based on his speech but based on a more in-depth study of Kalam's work in leadership as well. This is appropriate in the toolkit as Kalam is not only the one who reached the top, but he was also a project leader in one sense. He played a pivotal project leadership role in his tenure with the Defense Research and Development Organization (DRDO) and Indian Space and Research Organization (ISRO). We certainly deal with important projects that can affect the

161

profitability of the company or customer base. But the projects which Kalam lead are of utmost substantial that can change the course of the economy of a nation. He was leading the **Space Program of ISRO**, particularly the **Launch Vehicle** aspect, **Agni Long-range Missile** of **DRDO**, and **PURA** - Providing Urban amenities in Rural Areas. Kalam succeeded as a project leader amid many challenges and changing ecosystems. Hence the leadership needed for driving such projects is intense, and there are quite a lot of which we can adopt in our day-to-day approaches for the projects. Kalam illustrated seven characteristics of a leader, which are very relevant for project leaders. Following are the seven cardinal rules inspired based on the essence of his speech to the project managers in a PMI conference.

1. A leader must have a vision
2. A leader must have a passion for transforming vision to action
3. A leader must deal with success and failures equally
4. Must have the courage to take a decision
5. A leader should have nobility in management
6. Every action of the leader should be transparent
7. The leaders should work with integrity and succeed with integrity

1. A LEADER MUST HAVE A VISION

A leader must possess a vision that is larger them himself. A leader should be able to see things that are unseen the others. This is the first and foremost characteristic of a project leader. Particularly a project leader, quite often he or she is given the task of creating a product service that was not existing, or there is no precedence to it. The ability to see a product that is not exciting yet, and inspire team members to see it as well as an essential habit of a project leader. This is the power of shared vision which they have seen in earlier chapters.

The ability of a project leader to embark on this vision among the team members makes the team aligned to its purpose and channelize their energy towards attaining the purpose becomes possible. No wonder why Kalam makes this is the first characteristic of a project leader. When India was lagging behind the space program, not even having the drawings of the launch vehicle and spacecraft prepared, Prof. Vikram Sarabhai had a vision of putting transponders in geostationary orbits. Today 160 transponders of India are in the orbit. While Kalam had Prof. Vikram Sarabhai and Prof. Swaminathan as a leader because of their ability to see the things which were not possible, every project leader has equal opportunity to inspire the project team to see the product or services which the project aims to deliver.

2. A LEADER MUST HAVE A PASSION FOR TRANSFORMING VISION TO ACTION

Passion is the one that transforms vision into action. While vision marks the true north of a journey, the passion makes one undertake the journey towards reaching the destination. The passion of the project leader ignites the energy and enthusiasm of the project team. This is one of the major factors that create the excitement and voluntary engagement of the project teams. This produces extraordinary results when it comes to the delivery of a project. Passion makes one enjoy the work and have the utmost satisfaction when the team delivers the product or service. The passion gives energy and enthusiasm for the team to work towards achieving the purpose of a project. A Leader must be able to walk in the unexplored path and be a role model for the teams to follow. And passion is the fuel that makes the leader propel the journey in the unexplored path.

3. A LEADER MUST DEAL WITH SUCCESS AND FAILURES EQUALLY

A leader's path cannot be filled with success alone, particularly in projects. Handling successes and failures with emotional fortitude is an essential trait of a project leader. Kalam gives an example of his leader, Dr. Satish Dhawan, in 1979 when he was the director of a Satellite Launch Vehicle, the mission failed to launch the satellite in the orbit. Yet as a Chairman of ISRO Dr. Dhawan assumed the responsibility for the failure, but later on, let his teams take the credit when it finally succeeded. The next mission was prepared and launched successfully in 1980, and then he asked Kalam to address the media and assume the responsibility for the success. This is one of the attitudes which inspired the entire team and created several leaders like Kalam himself.

Essentially in projects, leaders need to be prepared to handle failures as well as successes. The crux is rewarding the team for the achievements and handling failures such that the team as well as customers learn from them and utilize the learning in future projects.

Many times in today's world, we don't wait to see a project fail but make the course correction or critical decision to continue failing projects. We have difficulty in slaying a bleeding project due to the emotional attachment to it. Managing success is well done, but managing failure with emotional fortitude and full accountability is the essence of project leadership. Taking responsibility for the failure and put the team forward for success is indeed a habit of authentic project leadership.

> The day when a project manager owns failure on himself, he becomes a leader.

4. MUST HAVE THE COURAGE TO TAKE DECISION

A leader must have the courage to take decisions. Several decisions could go wrong. Out of a hundred, five fails, but must not be bogged down by the failure. The problem should not become the captain of our projects, but we should master the problems and defeat them. Management books cannot teach everything, one must learn from their experience to become the captain of the problem.

> Right or wrong, any decision is better than indecisiveness in projects.

Decisions, particularly timely decisions are the key ingredient that determines the success of the project. Specifically when the product life cycle is very short, and there is rapid technology obsolescence, the endurance of the product in the market space is determined by the timing of its launch. There are widespread examples for this in market space, which includes Nokia for not entering into the touch phone segment, and Kodak, which was clinging to its photo film technology. In projects as well, the major aspect that does not let the project progress is the ability to take a timely decision. Most of the projects are performed in a matrix organization, and there are several stakeholders to be involved in the decisions. The project leader must possess the authority to decide or at least be able to present this to the people who matter and influence them to take timely decisions.

5. LEADER SHOULD HAVE NOBILITY IN MANAGEMENT

A project leader needs to handle a lot of people and investment in every project, as put forth by Kalam, this need be dealt with nobility. Nobility is one of the strengths. Kalam gives an example of a leader whom he worked with, Dr. Bram Prakash – a noble soul but performer; he does not tolerate low performance, yet deal with everyone with empathy, dignity, and high standards.

Handling money is a critical aspect of the life of a project leader, and many times, the projects are capital intensive. Treating people such as employees, contractors, and partners is another important aspect. These two need to be approached with nobility.

Quite often in the project, many of these resources can be temporary as the project itself could be temporary. Hence not taking it for granted, but use the highest standards of fairness is indeed an essential trait. A project leader must celebrate the successes, reward exceptional performers in an unbiased manner. A project ecosystem is susceptible to the creation of silos and turf wars. But it is the project leader who converges everyone with the highest level of dignity, which makes the team proud to be associated with those projects and operate as a single moving organism.

In project managers' language, the 'critical path' to the success of a project leader is to help others to succeed.

---

6. EVERY ACTION OF THE LEADER SHOULD BE TRANSPARENT

Every action of the leader should be transparent. The team should know why the decisions are taken in such a way.

The transparency in information and decisions is an inherent trait that is needed by a leader, who is in that position to converge multiple teams to execute a project. Not having adequate information across the board hinders the progress of a project and dilutes the common vision and direction. A project leader must be transparent himself the various aspects of the project. As well as encourage the teams to be transparent enough within each other to have full access to the desired information about various aspects of the project.

7. THE LEADERS SHOULD WORK WITH INTEGRITY AND SUCCEED WITH INTEGRITY

This is one of the greatest qualities of a project leader as put forth by Kalam. Leading with integrity and succeeding with integrity is a prerequisite of the existence of the 21st century. As projects involve a lot of investment, resources, and brand equity of a company, the project leader must have integrity in every transaction. Integrity is an indispensable aspect of leading a project, and it must never be compromised. Kalam worked on public sector programs, he knew the intricacies, in his forty years of career in public service, no one has ever approached him for any malicious intention. This is possible when one creates a brand image like Kalam when it comes to ethics and integrity. A scrupulous image is essential for every project leader. Lead with integrity and succeed with integrity, is the tagline for any organization to thrive in this ecosystem.

When a leader follows these cardinal rules, they become one who inspires the team. They get things done not by power but by influencing people for accomplishments of their mission. They choose empowerment over authority. They exercise the vision to change from commander to coach, manager to mentor, director to delegator, hierarchy to synergy, seniority to creativity. These are APJ Abdul Kalam's words and what worked for him and must work for us as well.

Eight or Infinity?

Change is the only constant. – Heraclitus,

Greek philosopher

The single version of the truth is most substantial in projects. Everyone in the project team needs to have the same visibility of the objectives progress, decisions, and status. While this is the foundation aspect of any project, there is further to this to gain exact alignment on the projects. We have to go deeper to understand this.

Even a single version of the truth can be interpreted by various stakeholders in different ways from the perspectives from where they are looking at it. It is said that the word belongs to the speaker, and the meaning belongs to the one who hears them. Hence in today's context, where we have diverse groups with various cultural, technical, and geographical backgrounds, there is always a scope for a different interpretation of the same message.

If in real estate, it is about 'location-location-location,' then in projects it is about 'communication-communication-

171

communication". The following is an incident that demonstrates that this is not overstated.

Story 8: Story of API

It was a beautiful morning, and I, along with my colleague called upon an enthusiastic IT start-up company partner to our corporate office in order to discuss the possibility of making automated dashboards from various applications. You know, the Pharma domain is unique (as we seem to claim for all fields, I learned off late), and we would love to have someone who has a deep understanding of the domain to work with us. The partner claimed that he had already worked on a couple of assignments in this startup and as a part of a more extensive career from which he had begun this venture.

Moved by this, we went on discussing further. "what do you think a most critical success factor in such a pharma project" I asked. "API" the reply was spontaneous, "It is very complex to develop, and there are multiple moving parts, hence in my experience, there are many instances we are stumbling upon this, and we have to be extremely vigilant about this". We were stunned to look at the thorough understanding of an IT buddy in a complex domain like pharma.

The discussion went on, we discussed various strategies to control and risk mitigate API. At one point in time, when it became overwhelming, we started realizing that there is something drastically wrong with this conversation. The partner started saying many things which we have not heard before. Further probing proved that the API which he referred to having an entirely different meaning 'Application Programming Interface.' The API which we all had in our mind is 'Active Pharmaceutical Ingredient' is the ingredient of any drug that produces its effects.

Indeed, the partner had profound insights into API, the Application Programming Interface is a set of subroutine definitions, protocols, and tools for building application software. API still remains a significant challenge when integrating multiple bespoke software applications and trying to do something meaningful, such as what we were driving to accomplish, but the API which he spoke about and the API we had in mind are entirely different.

Communications could be tricky in a project environment. The first step towards more transparent communication is to pre-empt the use of jargon, abbreviations in the project meetings, or at least to qualify them whenever needed. Communication gaps can cause a difference in perspective, the real-life scenario is much more complicated than just avoiding abbreviations. Quite often, there are conflicts between teams or team members in projects. As tasks are performed for the first time, there will be different perspectives in which each other workstream or team player might perceive a situation. A project leader is the one who can converge them together and give them an unambiguous direction to progress towards the true north of the project.

Unlike the API story, my experience in many of the conflicting situations is that each other perspective is correct in their sense. And each of the stakeholders is correct from their point of you. The simple detection of this situation is how one sees the number 8 from different angles.

You might have seen the cartoon which illustrates two-person views the number 6 from a different angle, and one claims it is 6 and the other claims it is 9.

Similarly, just visualize an 8. The one who sees from the bottom would say that it is a number 8, the same structure looks like an infinity from a different angle. Both of them sees the same thing but perceive different meaning. Both of them are right. It is the perspectives, and the position from which each of them operates that makes individuals viewing the same things differently from their perspective. If not addressed early enough, these perspectives would become a strong belief and pave the

way for the creation of silos and turf wars. Some of the project leaders might evidence this between two important

workstreams which contribute to the success of the project. A project leaders' task is to have a consistent, ongoing dialogue between them to impel the project forward. A project leader is someone who finds perception issues early enough and brings them together so that both of them see the same thing in each other's perspectives.

This would be possible when the project leader possesses a larger vision. This could be tricky for the execution teams who are close to their tasks, as the one looks at eight as eight and the other eight as infinity. When someone looks from a bird's eye view, they can sense that both of them are right from their operating angle, and bring them to the same place would solve the conflict early enough.

While conflict resolution is an inevitable aspect of the life of a project leader, pre-empting such situations by making people operate from the same place is a proactive approach. This can be inculcated by being purpose-centric in projects. The aspect such as creating the shared vision, aligning the team towards the true north of the project, and being customer-centric brings them together early enough. When leaders understand the necessity of this and operate from the view that throngs people together break the barriers between workstreams to execute projects faster, make the teams work together better, and make the individuals who contribute to the projects.

Whenever there is a situation like this, ask a question, "Is it eight or infinity?" This will become a strong reminder for the project leaders to quickly recognize the difference in perspective and align the team.

CO-HOLDING THE PERSPECTIVES

People engaged in projects gathered from different geographies and workstreams. Hence they have different objectives and KPIs. But the project is a place where everyone has to come together with single-mindedness and perform to create a solution. Hence co-holding the perspectives is important for the individuals who perform the task. It's about the understanding that each of the other team members would see things differently, and would perceive results differently, yet have the respect for an individual's contribution and alignment towards the larger purpose which is intended to be created through those projects. The individual perceptions come secondary,

175

comparing two creating value through the project. This understanding and appreciation would glue the teams together and create synergy through the task execution towards the fulfillment of the project needs.

Tool

9

The Ninty-9 Rule: Rolling Wave Planning

"The nicest thing about not planning is that failure comes as a complete surprise rather than being preceded by periods of worry and depression." —Sir John Harvey-Jones

As a famous quote from Benjamin Franklin states, "If you fail to plan, you are planning to fail!". A project leader's core process is the planning and the way in which one makes this determines half of the success of the project even before it commences. Beginning with the purpose is the first step, it is an undeniable truth that the entire project needs to be planned for this purpose. Projects are different, there are several projects which might extend to years together; there are several projects which might complete within a couple of months. The question is how to focus on the progressively unveiled activities. Do we focus on the entire lifecycle at all times or focus on the immediate steps to achieve the purpose of the project?

Story 9: Sally's granular schedule

Sarah Williams joined the big pharmaceutical multinational corporation as head of program management. This corporation has been there for 67 years and has had several accolades for launching new products into the markets. Each of these products measures up to several billion dollars of business. And these products are indeed challenging to develop and launch in the market. One in a million ideas become a product. It gets screened through various phases of the product development lifecycle.

Every department in the company operated as an island of excellence. Though this was required by the nature of the business, as a by-product this also has created concrete silos between departments. Her first challenge is to put a system in place, which integrates all the stakeholders as a single moving entity towards creating the objectives of the program. She wanted to create a single project plan from beginning to end, which will help the organization to know the status of each project. She does not like to miss even a minute aspect that needs to be done. After a lot of struggle, thirty members from different workstreams came together and created a project schedule which has almost 2500 tasks, and the finish date of the generic schedule was impractical for any project. This was as a result of trying to micromanage the activities of each department, which created an explosion of activity.

There were two significant problems with that 'generic schedule' number one is it the project completion date which has given has been pushed out to a large extent comparing to the nominal timeline. Number two functions feel that they are being micromanaged

The ninety-9 cycle is designed to handle the progressively unveiled aspect of the project while aligning with the purpose of the project. This is a tool that is carved out from my other book, Spiral Staircase Project Management (Robert, 2017). There are three levels of planning.

- Directionally correct masterplan
- 90 days of tactical plan
- 9 days of the watertight execution schedule

Ninety-9 is about preparing a master plan of the project that gets recalibrated every ninety days to align with the purpose of the project. In line with ninety days plan, the granular execution schedule in 9 days cycle is prepared. The 9 days watertight schedules are targeted for ultimate speed in the execution. The ninty-9 planning provides a well-designed execution canvas for the projects.

At the initial stage of the project, a master plan that has various milestone which has to be achieved to attain the project objective is worked out. The same larger project plan can be made into granular pieces every 9 days. This gives agility and control as the project progresses. The 9 days detailed planning covers a week's activity and two more days majorly. This is to be done at the beginning of every week and helps to cover all the near-term activities.

You don't have to see the whole staircase, just take your first step, the rest will be shown to you.

-Martin Luther King Junior

A good metaphor for this is a rolling wave of the ocean. The wave has water that is calm at far, and while approaching the terminal, it is turbulent. Similarly, the masterplan is worked out with high-level milestones, with broader assumptions, risks, and issues. But while approaching the execution point, the same is detailed into granular 9 days schedule, as most of the assumptions can be translated into specific actions. Disambiguation of the assumptions, manifestation of risks would have happened then. Hence it is appropriate to work out a detailed actionable schedule.

PROCESS: INITIAL PLANNING— CREATE A MASTER PLAN

Every project has a purpose to be achieved, this could be the creation of the results, services, or products. The first step of any project before planning is to define this. The next step is to build a master plan that is designed to deliver the purpose. A master plan is a high-level, directionally correct plan that is to be carried out to achieve the project's objectives. Every project has a core flow—the set of sequential segments that are to be performed one after another, towards the final objectives. Defining the core flow is the first step in preparing a project master plan.

A master plan can be an approximately right schedule where the accuracy of estimates is not the objective—it is a reflection of this core flow, and its progress represents the overall progress of the project. Once the purpose and core flow are worked out, they are divided into several logical segments. We call them 'stages.' Activities to be performed in a stage comprises several steps. Detailing out this is synonymous to work breakdown structure (WBS) in traditional methodology. Every stage has to deliver intermittent objectives, which have to be accomplished one after another to deliver the purpose of the larger project. Time, cost, and intermediate milestones are to be defined at every stage. The following criteria can be used to work out the stages

a.   Where the project can be logically divided into segments: *An example is of analysis, development, test, and release in a typical software development project.*

b.   Where a significant delivery can happen—*such as the development of proof of concept.*

c.   Where there is a transition from one workstream to another, *such as a research team to the production team.*

d.   Where there is a transfer of knowledge from one individual or workstream to another, *such as outsourcing part of the project to an external vendor/ partner.*

The number of stages in a project solely depends on the nature of the project, rigor of execution, and quality of decision-making needed. The purpose becomes the core objective, and the flow of the project towards achieving this purpose is represented in the master plan. The milestones and intermediate deliveries are to be chosen in such a way that they represent the overall health of the project. Hence, the focus should be on the flow of the project rather than time—using the compass rather than a clock to detail the steps of the project's progress.

Traditionally, at the planning stage, the target is to have an accurate schedule by working out a detailed set of deliverables. There are also numerous assumptions, risks, and workaround strategies attached to the plan. However, the more granular the plan, the more inaccurate it will be due to the 'snowballing effects' of the inaccuracies towards the end. This happens because the planning is made in the early stages of the project, with very low visibility of the future, and leads to rigidity in the system. The steps are not detailed in a granular manner at this stage, except for the first ninety days. As the project is progressively revealed, one may not know the intricacies concealed in further steps, and the accuracy of detailing of each milestone would be better achieved after completing the previous one. Hence, the master plan can only be a gross plan of the project, which will help in predicting upfront requirements approximately, not accurately. The nominal timeline required to accomplish every stage, and the resources necessary are also worked out at this point in time. Hence, a master plan gives 40,000 feet view of the time, cost, and resources needed to complete a project and deliver its core purpose. This is to facilitate a feasibility check and lining up resources.

While aligning with the purpose of the project at every stage of the project is essential through the vision map, it also has clearly laid out criteria for go/no-go decisions. For example, the purpose may be to develop a product that has a specific drop-dead date for it to be successful. Often, these products have exclusive marketing rights or tax incentives only if it is delivered on such date. In such a case, time becomes the true north. If another product is launched or the project is missing the time of a tax incentive, the feasibility of the product undergoes a major revision. Such aspects need to be defined as upfront as 'go or kill' criteria.

Assumptions are to be validated every ninety days. Various external factors are to be checked at every step, including regulation changes, technology upgrades, competitors' launches, and changes in customer requirements.

Depending on the project management maturity of the organization, all the other best practices like communication management, procurement management also need to be worked out. Excellence can be learned from unexpected quarters of life, here for project leaders, the Dabbawalas indicate the simplicity in the planning process would result in excellence in delivery.

90 DAYS OF TACTICAL EXECUTION PLAN

The project execution approach in this methodology is to systematically convert the master plan into accurate, actionable mini-projects, deliver them with increased value and velocity, and align them to the purpose. In the master plan stage, the project is divided into several segments; at the execution stage, it is carried out quarterly. Most of the projects have gone through the earlier stages, the level of predictability would be relatively larger for the next ninety days at any point in time in the project. Resources and cost estimation would be more accurate while doing a ninety days plan. Hence, the approach here is to develop more detailed schedules, which is highly probable for the next ninety days. Every quarter has inputs, processes, and outputs, and is similar to mini-projects such as development, production, testing, and releasing. The output gained at the completion of a milestone becomes the input for the subsequent milestone. While completing every quarter, overall timing and cost need to be recalibrated based on the progress of the current quarter.

There are four steps for the execution of each milestone—focus, plan, process, and move on.

A detailed schedule can be prepared for the first ninety days. When finishing the first quarter, the second quarter is conspicuous —hence, assemble the project team and work out a more detailed plan for the second quarter. Do the same for subsequent milestones and continue this iteration until the project's objective is delivered.

Quarterly project reviews facilitate business reviews of the project at regular intervals. This ensures the project sponsor's alignment and commitment to further resources. While proceeding with a project, there may be many changes in the customer and business environment concerning strategic, operational, and tactical elements—a project is not insulated from these even though it is being executed on that assumption. Often, the project teams are unprepared to take into account all these changes as this gets checked at the end of the project at the time of product delivery. Sometimes the team realizes that the product is no longer viable for the market. This is a better situation comparing to launching in the market and becoming unsuccessful. This is due to the lack of systemic, consistent calibration of the product viability after the initial assessment in the entire project lifecycle. Hence the quarterly review is designed for doing this. Take stock of the external and government regulations, and get to know the profile of the competitors and customers, if the project is more consumer- or technology-oriented, to factor in the refinements in the project plan. Sometimes, significant course corrections may be needed. All this depends on the extent to which the project is influenced by the above-said factors. Sometimes this will lead to go/kill decisions—pruning a project in the early stages is better rather than progressing until the end and realizing that it is no more viable. This way, resources, and investment can be diverted to feasible projects. While terminating a project is an extreme measure and may not happen quite often, this review will help in finer adjustments to meet the ultimate goal. Pressure testing the assumptions made at an earlier stage can result in mitigation options to carry out the project seamlessly.

While this is mainly focused on forward-looking aspects, the quarterly reviews can also be effective in pressure testing the quality and rigor of execution. This helps the project team evaluate the progress thus far and ensure that the deliverables are fully accomplished before moving on to the next quarter. Also, this validates the assumptions and enables a choice of mitigation options for some of the risks foreseen earlier. At the end of a quarterly review, the performance report— that covers the project's performance up to this quarter, project metrics, projections, and variance report—needs to be reported to ensure that the current status of the project is communicated to the stakeholders.

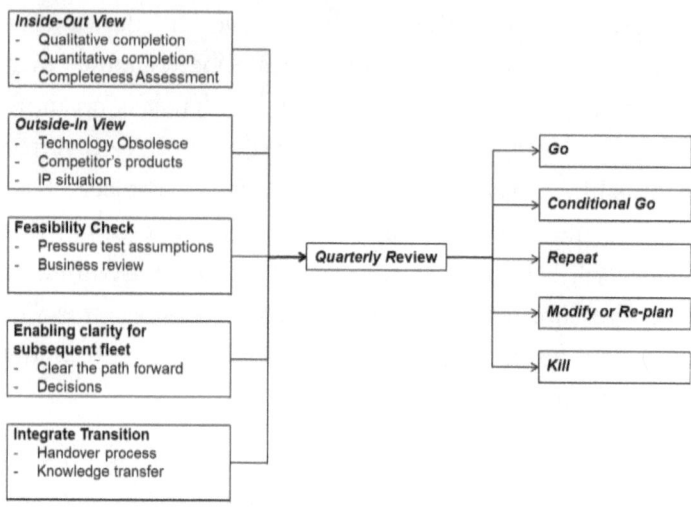

Figure 16: Quarterly Reviews

9 DAYS EXECUTION MODEL

This is where the rubber meets the road. The master plan helps in creating the vision, and the quarterly plan sets the direction of the project towards the purpose, the 9 days watertight schedule aims at the execution by making a more granular plan which is precisely planned and accurately executed.

Watertight schedules

A 'watertight schedule' is defined as a schedule that is so meticulously planned with highly probable steps, which is impossible to defeat. Preparing this upfront for an entire project is not suggested due to various known-unknowns and unknown-unknowns at the beginning of the project. However, it is possible to prepare for a granular level schedule under the following circumstances:

a.   Having completed all the penultimate activities of project

b.   Successfully passing through a quarterly review, which provides the 'go-ahead' signal to proceed with the next steps

c.   Subsequent steps are progressively unveiled

d.   All assumptions can be validated and converted into concrete action items

e.   There is no ambiguity in the actions and decisions needed to perform activities of the next steps

For simplicity, we can classify the events in a project into two categories—tasks and idle time. Tasks can be broadly classified into two categories—variable and non-variable tasks. The duration of variable tasks can be altered by the number of resources deployed in executing the tasks. Sometimes, they can be shortened by deploying additional resources, investment, or methods of execution. If an activity can be done in ten days by one resource, and in five days with two resources, this is a variable task. These tasks can help in shortening or extending a deliverable, depending on the criticality of the deliverable. Also, this can be modulated to optimize the cost of the tasks. Non-variable tasks cannot be shortened by deploying additional resources and require a fixed duration of time to accomplish these tasks.

A simple analogy is traveling from one place to another—it takes ten hours by road, thirty minutes by flight. The duration of the task is determined by the speed needed for this particular activity and relative investment. The cost and time can be balanced to see how fast it needs to move

187

along with the overall milestone speed—hence, it is a variable task. In real-world projects, this is similar to having multiple dedicated teams, hi-tech equipment, and automated technology to deliver more precise and faster products versus alternate time-consuming processes. The duration of non-variable tasks cannot be altered by increasing resources or by any other means. A good analogy for this is the incubation time for product testing. If a product needs to be incubated for six months in stability chambers to see if there is an impact on product quality over time, the time cannot be shortened by splitting it and putting it into more than one stability chamber. Hence, the duration of the non-compressible tasks remains static. On the other hand, there are idle times that are planned, as well as forced by the type of tasks. 'Planned idle time' occurs when the team waits for a key input or material or a predecessor to complete, and 'forced idle time' is by virtue of the task's nature.

A watertight schedule has a series of tasks and idle time one after another, both sequential and parallel, in accordance with the network of the project milestone. In an optimum schedule, the variable tasks help in playing around with the resources to shorten or extend the duration. One cannot do anything about the non-variable tasks and idle time, but some activities can be planned in parallel so that there is progress even during idle time.

If a milestone is to be delivered fast or cost-efficient, the same needs to be worked out based on the nature of the milestone. For instance, for products that have high technology obsolescence but a rich margin, time is essential. Hence, the use of additional resources and investment needed to complete the milestone at the earliest should be the approach. If a project is targeted for cost leadership, the watertight schedule can be made in accordance with the cost.

The progress of the project is to be measured in accordance with the advancement of the tasks and idle time consumption. The tasks that result in progress are the ones that lead to the project's progress. These have a direct correlation between effort and effect. Often, some tasks do not result in progress after the first few iterations but will ultimately get completed. The last iteration, which results in the effect, represents the progress. Hence, when multiple iterations are needed to produce the desired results, it is useful to deploy the available bench strength resources to expedite the progress of the current milestone. This, in effect, results in an improvement in the overall project.

Tool

0

Bonus Tool

Success is going from failure to failure without
loss of enthusiasm - Winston Churchill

The Bonus Tool: The Zero Mistake is a tool that disillusions the first-time-right expectation. Zero mistakes are seldom feasible in the complex project ecosystem that we operate today. A project ecosystem is a mistake-prone environment. Hence the approach is not to be mistake averse but to leverage mistakes for learning. This orientation adds immense value to the organizations. It is about dealing with uncertainties and risks, hence there need for tolerance for mistakes, learn from the errors.

You might have probably known a classic parable using a pencil. The author of the pencil–parable is unknown, but with due regards to him, we have represented the parable herewith. The parable goes like how God created man for a purpose, but let us stick to the third verse of this parable. While making a pencil, it is attached with an eraser. This is because the student or the artist who uses the pencil is bound to make mistakes. Hence the eraser comes as a

191

handy correction tool for the one which can potentially create the mistake. Making a mistake is an integral part of creativity. The more mistakes an artist makes with a pencil make she perfect, a seasoned artist. If the artist wants the first time right, we may not have so many artists evolved in this world. Fear of failure is the first thing that blocks the creative process. Similarly, people in several fields are bound to make mistakes. The difference between winner and loser is the one who has the ability and courage to correct the mistakes and move on in life.

While the entire nine tools we have seen so far are the things that need to be done, but this bonus tool is something that we should not expect from the project team. Uncertainty and unpredictability are an inherent part of projects. Many times, we stumble upon a situation that the expectation is the project teams need to carry out tasks the first time right, every time. This would have been possible two decades ago, but for a cognitive innovation project, the ability of the team to take the risk, and execute the project in the right stride is a requirement to make progress on the project.

Expecting zero error and punishing for mistakes make the team operate cautiously and in a conservative mode. This stifles the thinking process, impedes innovation, reduce risk appetite, decelerate the decision making and thus result in slowing down the speed of execution. People would become more sensitive about mistakes and hence will not take chances, which will slow down the progress. A child learns to walk by making several mistakes. She falls again and again. Every fall leads to the rise of the child; every mistake makes the walk perfect.

- A mistake by a scientist becomes an invention
- The mistake by a poet makes a sonnet
- The mistake in pottery becomes an artwork
- The mistake by a chef gives rise to a unique dish
- A mistake in a decision becomes a valuable lesson

Mistakes are an essential component of a learning curve. We learn not to touch fire from other's experiences or sometimes we experiment ourselves to gain knowledge. Others or our own, either way, mistakes lead us towards perfection.

Sony corporation's first products - rice cooker was a failure, Boeing's first seaplane failed. However, these companies build their empire in continuous learning and now became a household name. In Today's fast-paced and cut-throat competitive project ecosystem, we tend to have no tolerance for mistakes, every effort target for the first time right every time. Ironically every breakthrough innovation is made through an iterative, evolving process.

Contrary to what we see today, research evidenced that there are fewer breakthrough innovations that happened in this century. All the new products we are seeing are an extension of the application or the product enhancements and not radical inventions. The philosophy of making the first time right indeed stifles the creative thinking process.

If you closely analyze unsuccessful attempts at developing breakthrough products, perhaps the most common trouble you find is not one of the usual suspects, such as lack of top-management

> *commitment. Instead, you'll see that efficiency-minded*
> *project managers are inadvertently discouraging the*
> *explorations – and therefore the learning – that*
> *make radical ideas practical. (Lorenz, 2013)*

The invention of the wheel, the internet, the computer, electricity is some things which changed how human lives on this blue planet. Such inventions are becoming scarce now. Every breakthrough innovation created a leap of improvement in the quality of life.

Kindling the playful energy in the project teams is necessary, particularly for the knowledge era projects. The world which I evidenced – the pharmaceutical industry had many inventions a couple of decades ago compared to today. One of the reasons articulated for the decline in innovation in big pharmaceutical corporations and new products is because of following the *'efficiency centric management practices.'* Research centers started adapting to the triple constraints of time, cost, and scope and measure the success and failure of the projects. This is an effort that affected the creative thinking of the scientist as the analytical framework does not provide the necessary leverage for them to invent. Even in the other industries, we see the start-ups which do not have hard and fast rules coming up with new products rapidly but not the big conglomerate as it did a decade before.

Dan Pink, in his work, explains the world belongs to the creators and emphasizers, and the world is going to be dependent on this. All that we live in today is a benefit of the inventions made earlier and through their successes and failures. Are we doing the same level of contribution to humanity?

Willingness to make mistakes is a tremendous potential for development. If one hesitates to make a mistake and restrict herself for the first time right, she will end up waiting for an opt moment. When the opt moment comes up, it might be already late. Novel ideas, innovation evolve when a culture that fosters trial and error approaches towards the invention of new products. Unwillingness to make mistakes ends the risk appetite and prevents growth.

It is said that if one has not failed two times in their efforts, it is hard to get the venture capitalist funding any project in Silicon Valley. 'Fail fast and fail often' is almost a mantra in Silicon Valley. There are in fact, annual conferences and experience sharing sessions in the technology hubs where entrepreneurs deliver speeches about their misfires. A diverse version of the same concept happens in other technology hubs as well like Tokyo and Barcelona to name a few.

In the information era, we use human intelligence, information, and artificial intelligence to our advantage rather than relying on machinery. In every shift in human evolution, there is a courageous act of going against conventional wisdom, which makes humanity step on to the next logical progression. The one which might have been seen as the weird act may be the foundation for growth. Willingness to experiment, willingness to make a mistake has been the most significant intellectual capability which human have. This is the unique attribute that made them progress to the extent of ruling the world. Getting out of their comfort zone, breaking the conventional practices made humans achieve the impossible.

195

The perfectionist world

Great scientist, engineers, inventors, and philosophers are all the one who is not afraid of making mistakes. They never had to restrict their creative energy and think outside the box, which enabled them to come up with ideas that turned the way in which humans ever lived in this land. For this book I have been researching various of these successful people of the past, no one got through their effort in the first attempt. Their endeavors evidence that the failures are not the opposite of success, but a part of the success.

THE POST-IT

3Ms post-it is a highly quoted example of how a mistake can be turned into a successful product. When it was accidentally invented, this temporary nature of the adhesive was rejected. However, the application of the same was not realized then. Today this has become a product that is a ubiquitous piece of stationery in every office worldwide.

THE QUICK AND DIRTY PROGRAM

The entire computer programming was founded on a quick and dirty program. When Bill Gates was asked to write an operating system for IBMs personal computer, he had a small window of opportunity to found an empire that will change the way in which the computing world operates. All that he had is a limited time and a chance to establish his empire. The quick and dirty program paved the way for long-lasting success and became a perfect starting point for the field of computer operating system and programming

196

INTEL'S MISTAKE DAY

Intel conducts annual conferences to talk about the mistakes. Be hungry, be foolish – is the tagline of Steve Jobs in one of the convocation addresses. This is applicable to any project work as well. Encouraging out-of-the-box thinkers and giving space for them to experiment with small ideas is the way to progress and reap the benefits from this ecosystem. This is a lever for cognitive works, consider this as a must-have rather than nice to have, particularly if your projects needed breakthrough ideas and innovation.

Failure is not the opposite of success, it's part of success." - Arianna Huffington, co-founder, and editor-in-chief of The Huffington Post

---

New Ways of Working

Following are some of the new rules of engagement you can inculcate to accelerate the leadership journey of yourself as well as the project teams. These can be done as low-key affairs in the organizations at the early stages of the maturity continuum. If the organization is in the advanced stages, then this can be propagated to create a new way of working.

CREATE A COMPELLING TAGLINE FOR EVERY PROJECT

While the project charter and other document are prepared at the beginning of the project, there is nothing like having a compelling tagline which connects to the execution team to the vision of the project. This can be prominently displayed everywhere in order to connect the people to the purpose of the project. The compelling tagline needs to address the value the project is intended to create and connects people's contribution towards achieving this. This can be a defining statement that relates to the customer. This invokes the passion of the people and encourages them towards the purpose the project creates

Numbers are not necessarily inspiring, by providing project targets with numbers such as complete this within this time and with the budget may not be able to connect to the people who are executing the projects. Creating a compelling tagline that is connected to the contribution of every individual in adding value to the customer or the organization will be able to connect people towards the purpose of the project.

198

If a project does not have a compelling purpose, it may not worth pursuing. Be it creating value to the customer, generating new market space, a next-generation product, building a megastructure, creating new products for the company, several of such intents helps organizations to create a compelling vision.

INVOKE A LEARNING ORGANIZATION RATHER THAN MISTAKE-PROOF CULTURE

A mistake-proof culture limits the learning ability of the organization. Moreover, it does not allow issues to surface out quickly for immediate resolution. People tend to suppress the issues, and the ability of the project teams to implement course corrections swiftly may not be feasible. Remember the bullwhip effect. Course corrections made in the early stage are better than later as the impact would be multiplied at later stages. 'Everything needs to be done perfectly' is an expectation that brings in inflexibility, and people are always under pressure to deliver right the first time. Mistakes are bound to happen whether we accept them or not. Rather than making a system that does not have tolerance for errors, make the organization and project teams a learning entity. At least this ensures that people learn from the mistakes in order not to repeat the same in the same project or subsequent projects. This, over time benefits in increasing the reliability of the project team. This is how a mistake can be reduced, not by punishing.

FOSTER ENTREPRENEURS' CULTURE THAN EMPLOYEE CULTURE IN PROJECT TEAMS

The creative process needs an entrepreneur's mindset instead of the employee mindset. Projects are unique and one-time effort, hence involve a lot of ideation in it. Particularly, for the knowledge era, where the cognitive ability influences project's success. Some organizations call their employees partners, this reinstates the importance of the entrepreneurship of employees in creating value for the project as well as organizations. When the project team member becomes partners in the project in a real sense, they connect the shared vision, and the ownership and accountability increase multifold. One who is working on saving his/her job will not be able to create value for the organization. But the one who is with an entrepreneur mindset can create products, services, and results in an unprecedented rate.

TASK-ORIENTED TO GOAL-ORIENTED

Task orientation is the conventional approach toward controlling a project. In effect, there are situations where the tasks are tightly controlled, but the project is not approaching the end goal. Modern leadership focuses on the goals. A shift from the cause to the effect. Any task which is undertaken, if that creates value for the project and advances the project towards completion, is the true measure of the progress. 'I have done my job' is not going to help the project progress.

A parable that demonstrates this is about two contracts working on a highway. One contractor dug holes alongside a road and another one after sometimes came with his tools and filled it with dirt. While asking, they reported that they are doing their job, but another contractor who is supposed to show up in between both of them is needed to plant saplings in the hole, is not reported for the duty. This might look like a weird example, but in reality, when not focused on goals, but merely on tasks, in projects, we end up in such a situation.

'THINKING' PROJECT TEAMS THAN 'CHASING' PROJECT TEAMS

A chasing project team operates from a background of meeting the targets such as time, cost, and scope. A thinking project team is the one who keeps an eye on the very purpose the project needs to create. A thinking project team is the one who always sees the opportunity to add value to the project and eventually to the customers. It has a greater connection with market needs and user experience. Every task of the project is aligned with the larger mission and in the direction of the true north. When something is not in synchrony with the true north, the thinking culture enables a course correction head-on instead of deviating for a long time and firefighting. This eventually ends up achieving time, cost, and scope yet produces surpassing products, services, or results that will subsequently benefit customers.

FROM SCOPE CENTRIC TO PURPOSE CENTRIC

The scope should be ideally the reflection of the purpose of the project. Unfortunately, it is not always that way. The purpose centricity can bring in value-based thinking in every workstream involved in the project. The bottom line is purpose focus benefits the project teams and customers.

FROM PROBLEM ORIENTATION TO SOLUTION ORIENTATION

Sometimes you may observe that the project team is passionate about dwelling on the problems. The critical shift which is needed is to be a part of the solutions culture. This means effectively engaged in finding the solution to the issues that might evolve from time to time and keep the ball rolling towards achieving the desired outcomes. This solution orientation comes from resolving issues, finding facts, and putting progress on the front burner. Problem orientation is characterized by exposing people to be blamed, on the contrary, a solution orientation makes people think 'what' needs to be solved rather than 'whose fault is it.'

Afterword

The question is, does 'knowing' these tools adequate to upgrade a project manager to a leader level? The answer is, 'No.' It is indeed, the 'practice' of correct things makes perfect. The more one practice and uses these tools, the better he or she will become. The underlying assumption in this entire book is that the project managers have the necessary training on the basic framework of project management and have expertise in all 10 knowledge areas of project management.

You have been already honed the skills to deliver the projects on time, within cost, and scope. The toolset works with all the analytical frameworks to make the project more effective. So, one can focus on the journey towards leadership by augmenting the already acquired or learned experienced skills with the following

- Value your core values
- Prioritize your real priorities
- Trust your people
- Clarify the real purpose
- Focus on your customer

The beauty of these processes is one need not wait for anybody's approval in order to get started. This is more of an inward journey, which one can shift from the management side to the leadership side. Instead of changing the entire world, changing the individual is the first step in the process. It is indeed the individual to take a first step towards the leadership journey which will intern catalyst the cultural transformation. This toolset will undoubtedly provide a competitive advantage to the project leader to drive her project forward. These will reinforce the metamorphosis process of becoming a better leader and will be able to raise in the complex knowledge workers era of today. That's my promise.

List of illustration

Picture 1: The Cause and Effect Focus

Picture 2: The tree of project leadership

Figure 3: Project ecosystem of various ages

Figure 4: The Iron Triangle of Projects

Figure 5: Yardsticks of the Triple constraints

Figure 6: Focus of Manager and Leader

Figure 7: The Opportunity Triangle

Figure 8: Project Vision Board

Figure 9: Yardsticks of the Opportunity Triangle

Figure 10: The Project Leadership Diamond

Figure 11: RACI Chart

Figure 12: Issues and Decisions Flow in Meetings

Figure 13: Transforming Triple Constraints from Control Paradigm to Opportunity Paradigms

Figure 14: The Four ups

Figure 15: The Project Governance Maturity Model

Figure 16: Quarterly Reviews

Bibliography

Covey, S. R. (2004). *The 7 Habits of Highly Effective People.* Free Press; Revised edition (November 9, 2004).

Klein, G. (Sep 2007). Performing a Project Premortem. *Harvard Business Review.*

Lorenz, M. (2013). *How Good Management Stifles Breakthrough Innovation.* Harward Business Review.

Martin, D. (2009). *Secrets of the marketing masters: what the best marketers doand why it works.* Amacom.

Morris, P. W. (2013). *Reconstructing project management.* Cambridge, MA:: John Wiley.

Pink, D. H. (2008). *Drive : The Surprising Truth About What Motivates Us.* Riverhead Books.

PMI. (2018). *Pulse of the Profession 2018.* Project Management Institute .

Robert, J. (2017). *Spiral Staircase Project Management.* Notion Press.

Robert, J. (2017). *Spiral Staircase Project Management: A Framework to Succeed Complex-Cognitive Projects.* Chennai: Notion Press.

Yves Pigneur, G. B. (2015). *Value Proposition Design: How to Create Products and Services Customers Want.* Wiley.

Acknowledgments

Leadership in projects has been one of my passion and I am witnessing this change happening every day. Thanks to all my colleagues and network who are striving towards obtaining excellence in projects. None of this would have been possible without the experience I had in the corporate world. I'm eternally grateful to all the organizations I have associated with and the project teams I have worked with, in the past two decades. I truly have no idea if I would have written a book on leadership without the challenges which I have faced along with my team in executing projects and constructing PMOs.

My gratitude to Mike Teiler for editing several of the stories provided in this book. I am grateful to Eminence Business Media for launching this book in India in a project management conference, it can't get better than launching such a book among the like-minded professionals.

Nobody has been more important to me in the pursuit of this project than the members of my family. To Santhana Mary, Sheron, and Thanya: for always being my backbone in the writing part of my career and the other passion, wildlife photography. You are the people I could turn to during challenging times. So thankful to have you in my life.

About the Author

John Robert is a project leadership enthusiast with two decades of experience in projects, engineering, and operations. He has significant exposure in large-scale infrastructure projects and complex research program management. John is an engineer and MBA by education. He has 360degree exposure as a consultant, project manager, leader, and contractor, from a simple brick and mortar projects to ERP implementation to complex research and development programs.

While many of the projects he executed or lead were successful; he also had his share of failures. He considers his experience of challenging projects are more valuable, the projects that have not met the time, cost and scope targets. Many of them failed in spite of adopting the best practices of project management. His quest is in search of a solution to this; you will find this reflected in his writings. He uses metaphors that simplify the concepts to make the ideas simple, including his first book Spiral Staircase Project Management.

He can be contacted through email (johnrobert99@gmail.com) or LinkedIn (https://www.linkedin.com/in/johnrobertmanuel)

Also by the Author:

Spiral Staircase Project Management: A Framework to Succeed Complex-Cognitive Projects

Projects @ Relay Race: Deliver projects faster than you have imagined